Bait and Switch

Bait and Switch

The (Futile) Pursuit of the
American Dream

Barbara Ehrenreich

METROPOLITAN BOOKS
Henry Holt and Company ▪ New York

Metropolitan Books
Henry Holt and Company, LLC
Publishers since 1866
175 Fifth Avenue
New York, New York 10010
www.henryholt.com

Metropolitan Books® and ® are registered trademarks of
Henry Holt and Company, LLC.

Library of Congress Cataloging-in-Publication Data

Ehrenreich, Barbara.
    Bait and switch : the (futile) pursuit of the American dream /
Barbara Ehrenreich.—1st ed.
        p. cm.
    ISBN-10: 0-8050-7606-9
    ISBN-13: 978-0-8050-7606-6
    1. Displaced workers—United States. 2. White collar workers—
United States 3. Job hunting—United States. 4. Downward mobility
(Social sciences)—United States. I. Title.

HD5708.55.U6E47 2005
654.14'086'22—dc22   2005047916

    Henry Holt books are available for special promotions and
    premiums. For details contact: Director, Special Markets.

First Edition 2005

Designed by Kelly S. Too

Printed in the United States of America
1   3   5   7   9   10   8   6   4   2

contents

author's note

Most names in this book have been changed in the interest of privacy. The exceptions, in the majority of cases, are public speakers who were introduced by name and people I interviewed who agreed to have their full names used.

Bait and Switch

Introduction

Because I've written a lot about poverty, I'm used to hearing from people in scary circumstances. An eviction notice has arrived. A child has been diagnosed with a serious illness and the health insurance has run out. The car has broken down and there's no way to get to work. These are the routine emergencies that plague the chronically poor. But it struck me, starting in about 2002, that many such tales of hardship were coming from people who were once members in good standing of the middle class—college graduates and former occupants of mid-level white-collar positions. One such writer upbraided me for what she saw as my neglect of hardworking, virtuous people like herself.

> Try investigating people like me who didn't have babies in high school, who made good grades, who work hard and don't kiss a lot of ass and instead of getting promoted or paid

fairly must regress to working for $7/hr., having their student loans in perpetual deferment, living at home with their parents, and generally exist in debt which they feel they may never get out of.

Stories of white-collar downward mobility cannot be brushed off as easily as accounts of blue-collar economic woes, which the hard-hearted traditionally blame on "bad choices": failing to get a college degree, for example, failing to postpone childbearing until acquiring a nest egg, or failing to choose affluent parents in the first place. But distressed white-collar people cannot be accused of fecklessness of any kind; they are the ones who "did everything right." They earned higher degrees, often setting aside their youthful passion for philosophy or music to suffer through dull practical majors like management or finance. In some cases, they were high achievers who ran into trouble precisely because they had risen far enough in the company for their salaries to look like a tempting cost cut. They were the losers, in other words, in a classic game of bait and switch. And while blue-collar poverty has become numbingly routine, white-collar unemployment—and the poverty that often results—remains a rude finger in the face of the American dream.

I realized that I knew very little about the mid- to upper levels of the corporate world, having so far encountered this world almost entirely through its low-wage, entry-level representatives. I was one of them—a server in a national chain restaurant, a cleaning person, and a Wal-Mart "associate"—in the course of researching an earlier book, *Nickel and Dimed: On (Not) Getting By in America*. Like everyone else, I've also encountered the corporate world as a consumer, dealing with people quite far down in the occupational hierarchy—retail clerks, customer service representatives, telemarketers. Of the levels where decisions are made—where the vice presidents, account executives, and regional managers dwell—my experience has been limited to seeing these sorts of people on airplanes, where they study books on "leadership," fiddle with spreadsheets on their laptops, or fall asleep over biographies of the founding fathers.[1] I'm better acquainted with the corporate functionaries of the future, many of whom I've met on my visits to college campuses, where "business" remains the most popular major, if only because it is believed to be the safest and most lucrative.[2]

But there have been growing signs of trouble—if not outright misery—within the white-collar corporate workforce. First, starting with the economic downturn of 2001, there has been a rise in unemployment among highly credentialed and experienced people. In late 2003, when I started this project, unemployment was running at about 5.9 percent, but in contrast to earlier economic downturns, a sizable portion—almost 20 percent, or about 1.6 million—of the unemployed were white-collar professionals.[3] Previous downturns had disproportionately hit blue-collar people; this time it was the relative

1. Even fiction—my favorite source of insight into cultures and times remote from my own—was no help. While the fifties and sixties had produced absorbing novels about white-collar corporate life, including Richard Yates's *Revolutionary Road* and Sloan Wilson's *The Man in the Gray Flannel Suit*, more recent novels and films tend to ignore the white-collar corporate work world except as a backdrop to sexual intrigue.
2. National Center for Educational Statistics, http://nces.ed.gov/pubs2004/2004018.pdf.
3. According to the Bureau of Labor Statistics, women are only slightly more likely than men to be unemployed—6.1 percent compared to 5.7 percent—and white women, like myself, are about half as likely as black women to be unemployed (www.bls.gov).

elite of professional, technical, and managerial employees who were being singled out for media sympathy. In April 2003, for example, the *New York Times Magazine* offered a much-discussed cover story about a former $300,000-a-year computer industry executive reduced, after two years of unemployment, to working as a sales associate at the Gap.[4] Throughout the first four years of the 2000s, there were similar stories of the mighty or the mere midlevel brought low, ejected from their office suites and forced to serve behind the counter at Star-bucks.

Today, white-collar job insecurity is no longer a function of the business cycle—rising as the stock market falls and declining again when the numbers improve.[5] Nor is it confined to a few volatile sectors like telecommunications or technology, or a few regions of the country like the rust belt or Silicon Valley. The economy may be looking up, the company may be raking in cash, and still the layoffs continue, like a perverse form of natural selection, weeding out the talented and successful as well as the mediocre. Since the midnineties, this perpetual winnowing process has been institutionalized under various euphemisms such as "downsizing," "right-sizing," "smart-sizing," "restructuring," and "de-layering"—to which we can now add the outsourcing of white-collar functions to cheaper labor markets overseas.

---

4. Jonathan Mahler, "Commute to Nowhere," *New York Times Magazine,* April 13, 2003.
5. I was particularly enlightened by Jill Andresky Fraser's *White Collar Sweatshop: The Deterioration of Work and Its Rewards in Corporate America* (New York: Norton, 2001) and Richard Sennett's *The Corrosion of Character: The Personal Consequences of Work in the New Capitalism* (New York: Norton, 1998).

In the metaphor of the best-selling business book of the first few years of the twenty-first century, the "cheese"—meaning a stable, rewarding, job—has indeed been moved. A 2004 survey of executives found 95 percent expecting to move on, voluntarily or otherwise, from their current jobs, and 68 percent concerned about unexpected firings and layoffs.[6] You don't, in other words, have to lose a job to feel the anxiety and despair of the unemployed.

A second sign of trouble could be called "overemployment." I knew, from my reading, that mid- and high-level corporate executives and professionals today often face the same punishing demands on their time as low-paid wage earners who must work two jobs in order to make ends meet. Economist Juliet Schor, who wrote *The Overworked American,* and business journalist Jill Andresky Fraser, author of *White Collar Sweatshop,* describe stressed-out white-collar employees who put in ten- to twelve-hour-long days at the office, continue to work on their laptops in the evening at home, and remain tethered to the office by cell phone even on vacations and holidays. "On Wall Street, for example," Fraser reports, "it is common for a supervisor to instruct new hires to keep a spare set of clothes and toothbrush in the office for all those late night episodes when it just won't make sense to head home for a quick snooze."[7] She quotes an Intel employee:

If you make the choice to have a home life, you will be ranked and rated at the bottom. I was willing to work the endless

---

6. Harvey Mackay, *We Got Fired! And It's the Best Thing That Ever Happened to Us* (New York: Ballantine, 2004), p. 94.
7. Fraser, *White Collar Sweatshop,* p. 23.

hours, come in on weekends, travel to the ends of the earth. I
had no hobbies, no outside interests. If I wasn't involved with
the company, I wasn't anything.[8]

Something, evidently, is going seriously wrong within a so-
cioeconomic group I had indeed neglected as too comfortable
and too powerful to merit my concern. Where I had imagined
comfort, there is now growing distress, and I determined to investigate. I chose the same strategy I had employed in *Nickel
and Dimed*: to enter this new world myself, as an undercover
reporter, and see what I could learn about the problems firsthand. Were people being driven out of their corporate jobs?
What did it take to find a new one? And, if things were as bad
as some reports suggested, why was there so little protest?

The plan was straightforward enough: to find a job, a
"good" job, which I defined minimally as a white-collar position that would provide health insurance and an income of
about $50,000 a year, enough to land me solidly in the middle
class. The job itself would give me a rare firsthand glimpse into
the midlevel corporate world, and the effort to find it would of
course place me among the most hard-pressed white-collar
corporate workers—the ones who don't have jobs.

Since I wanted to do this as anonymously as possible, certain areas of endeavor had to be excluded, such as higher education, publishing (magazines, newspapers, and books), and
nonprofit liberal organizations. In any of these, I would have
run the risk of being recognized and perhaps treated
differently—more favorably, one hopes—than the average job

8. Fraser, *White Collar Sweatshop*, p. 158.

seeker. But these restrictions did not significantly narrow the field, since of course most white-collar professionals work in other sectors of the for-profit, corporate world—from banking to business services, pharmaceuticals to finance.

The decision to enter corporate life—and an unfamiliar sector of it, at that—required that I abandon, or at least set aside, deeply embedded attitudes and views, including my long-standing critique of American corporations and the people who lead them. I had cut my teeth, as a fledgling investigative journalist in the seventies, on the corporations that were coming to dominate the health-care system: pharmaceutical companies, hospital chains, insurance companies. Then, sometime in the eighties, I shifted my attention to the treatment of blue- and pink-collar employees, blaming America's intractable level of poverty—12.5 percent by the federal government's official count, 25 percent by more up-to-date measures—on the chronically low wages offered to nonprofessional workers. In the last few years, I seized on the wave of financial scandals— from Enron through, at the time of this writing, HealthSouth and Hollingers International—as evidence of growing corruption within the corporate world, a pattern of internal looting without regard for employees, consumers, or even, in some cases, stockholders.

But for the purposes of this project, these criticisms and reservations had to be set aside or shoved as far back in my mind as possible. Like it or not, the corporation is the dominant unit of the global economy and the form of enterprise that our lives depend on in a day-to-day sense. I write this on an IBM laptop while sipping Lipton tea and wearing clothes from the Gap—all major firms or elements thereof. It's corporations that make the planes run (though not necessarily on time), bring us (and increasingly grow) our food, and generally "make it happen." I'd been on the outside of the corporate world, often complaining bitterly, and now I wanted in.

THIS WOULD NOT, I knew, be an altogether fair test of the job market, if only because I had some built-in disadvantages as a job seeker. For one thing, I am well into middle age, and since age discrimination is a recognized problem in the corporate world even at the tender age of forty, I was certainly vulnerable to it myself. This defect, however, is by no means unique to me. Many people—from displaced homemakers to downsized executives—now find themselves searching for jobs at an age that was once associated with a restful retirement.

Furthermore, I had the disadvantage of never having held a white-collar job with a corporation. My one professional-level office job, which lasted for about seven months, was in the public sector, at the New York City Bureau of the Budget. It had involved such typical white-collar activities as attending meetings, digesting reports, and writing memos; but that was a long time ago, before cell phones, PowerPoint, and e-mail. In the corporate world I now sought to enter, everything would be new to me: the standards of performance, the methods of evaluation, the lines and even the modes of communication. But I'm a quick study, as you have to be in journalism, and counted on this to get me by.

The first step was to acquire a new identity and personal history to go with it, meaning, in this case, a résumé. It is easier to change your identity than you might think. Go to Alavarado and Seventh Street in Los Angeles, for example, and you will be approached by men whispering, "ID, ID." I, however, took the legal route, because I wanted my documents to be entirely in order when the job offers started coming in. My fear, perhaps exaggerated, was that my current name might be recognized, or would at least turn up an embarrassing abundance of Google entries. So in November 2003 I legally changed back to my maiden name, Barbara Alexander, and acquired a Social Security card to go with it.

As for the résumé: although it had to be faked, I wanted it as much as possible to represent my actual skills, which, I firmly believed, would enrich whatever company I went to work for. I am a writer—author of thousands of published articles and about twelve nonfiction books, counting the coauthored ones—and I know that "writing" translates, in the corporate world, into public relations or "communications" generally. Many journalism schools teach PR too, which may be fitting, since PR is really journalism's evil twin. Whereas a journalist seeks the truth, a PR person may be called upon to disguise it or even to advance an untruth. If your employer, a pharmaceutical company, claims its new drug cures both cancer and erectile dysfunction, your job is to promote it, not to investigate the grounds for these claims.

I could do this, on a temporary basis anyway, and have even done many of the things PR people routinely do: I've written press releases, pitched stories to editors and reporters, prepared press packets, and helped arrange press conferences. As an author, I have also worked closely with my publisher's PR people and have always found them to be intelligent and in every way congenial.

I have also been an activist in a variety of causes over the years, and this experience too must translate into something valuable to any firm willing to hire me. I have planned meetings and chaired them; I have worked in dozens of diverse groups and often played a leadership role in them; I am at ease as a public speaker, whether giving a lengthy speech or a brief presentation on a panel—all of which amounts to the "leadership" skills that should be an asset to any company. At the very least, I could claim to be an "event planner," capable of dividing gatherings into plenaries and break-out sessions, arranging the press coverage, and planning the follow-up events.

Even as a rough draft, the résumé took days of preparation. I had to line up people willing to lie for me, should they be called by a potential employer, and attest to the fine work I had done for them. Fortunately, I have friends who were willing to do this, some of them located at recognizable companies. Although I did not dare claim actual employment at these firms, since a call to their Human Resources departments would immediately expose the lie, I felt I could safely pretend to have "consulted" to them over the years. Suffice it to say that I gave Barbara Alexander an exemplary history in public relations, sometimes with a little event planning thrown in, and that the dissimulation involved in crafting my new résumé was further preparation for any morally challenging projects I should be called upon to undertake as a PR person.

I did not, however, embellish my new identity with an affect or mannerisms different from my own. I am not an actor and would not have been able to do this even if I had wanted to. "Barbara Alexander" was only a cover for Barbara Ehrenreich; her behavior would, for better or worse, always be my own. In fact, in a practical sense I was simply changing my occupational status from "self-employed/writer" to "unemployed"— a distinction that might be imperceptible to the casual observer. I would still stay home most days at my computer, only now, instead of researching and writing articles, I would be researching and contacting companies that might employ me. The new name and fake résumé were only my ticket into the ranks of the unemployed white-collar Americans who spend their days searching for a decent-paying job.

The project required some minimal structure; since I was stepping into the unknown, I needed to devise some guidelines for myself. My first rule was that I would do everything possible to land a job, which meant being open to every form of help that presented itself: utilizing whatever books, web sites, and businesses, for example, that I could find offering guidance to job seekers. I would endeavor to behave as I was expected to, insofar as I could decipher the expectations. I did not know exactly what forms of effort would be required of successful job seekers, only that I would, as humbly and diligently as possible, give it my best try.

Second, I would be prepared to go anywhere for a job or even an interview, and would advertise this geographic flexibility in my contacts with potential employers. I was based in Charlottesville, Virginia, throughout this project, but I was prepared to travel anywhere in the United States to get a job and then live there for several months if I found one. Nor would I shun any industry—other than those where I might be recognized—as unglamorous or morally repugnant. My third rule was that I would have to take the first job I was offered that met my requirements as to income and benefits.

I knew that the project would take a considerable investment of time and money, so I set aside ten months[9] and the sum of $5,000 for travel and other expenses that might arise in the course of job searching. My expectation was that I would make the money back once I got a job and probably come out far ahead. As for the time, I budgeted roughly four to six months for the search—five months being the average for unemployed people in 2004[10]—and another three to four months of employment. I would have plenty of time both to sample the life of the white-collar unemployed and to explore the corporate world they sought to reenter.

From the outset, I pictured this abstraction, *the corporate world,* as a castle on a hill—well fortified, surrounded by difficult checkpoints, with its glass walls gleaming invitingly from on high. I knew that it would be a long hard climb just to get to the door. But I've made my way into remote and lofty places before—college and graduate school, for example. I'm patient and crafty; I have stamina and resolve; and I believed that I could do this too.

In fact, the project, as I planned it, seemed less challenging than I might have liked. As an undercover reporter, I would of course be insulated from the real terrors of the white-collar work world, if only because I was independent of it for my income and self-esteem. Most of my fellow job seekers would probably have come to their status involuntarily, through layoffs or individual firings. For them, to lose a job is to enter a

---

9. From December 2003 to October 2004, with the exception of most of July, when I had a brief real-life job writing biweekly columns for the *New York Times.*
10. John Leland, "For Unemployed, Wait for New Work Grows Longer," *New York Times,* January 9, 2005.

world of pain. Their income collapses to the size of an unemployment insurance check; their self-confidence plummets. Much has been written about the psychological damage incurred by the unemployed—their sudden susceptibility to depression, divorce, substance abuse, and even suicide.[11] No such calamities could occur in my life as an undercover job seeker and, later, jobholder. There would be no sudden descent into poverty, nor any real sting of rejection.

I also started with the expectation that this project would be far less demanding than the work I had undertaken for *Nickel and Dimed*. Physically, it would be a piece of cake—no scrubbing, no heavy lifting, no walking or running for hours on end. As for behavior, I imagined that I would be immune from the constant subservience and obedience demanded of low-wage blue-collar workers, that I would be far freer to be, and express, myself. As it turns out, I was wrong on all counts.

11. See, for example, Katherine S. Newman's *Falling from Grace: Downward Mobility in the Age of Affluence* (Berkeley: University of California Press, 1999) or, for a highly readable first-person account, G. J. Meyer's *Executive Blues* (New York: Franklin Square Press, 1995).

one

Finding a Coach
in the Land of Oz

Where to begin? My first foray into the world of job searching, undertaken at my computer on a gloomy December afternoon, is distinctly intimidating. These days, I have gathered from a quick tour of relevant web sites, you don't just pore over the help-wanted ads, send off some résumés, and wait for the calls. Job searching has become, if not a science, a technology so complex that no mere job seeker can expect to master it alone. The Internet offers a bewildering variety of sites where you can post a résumé in the hope that a potential employer will notice it. Alternatively, you can use the net to apply directly to thousands of companies. But is the résumé eye-catching enough? Or would it be better to attempt face-to-face encounters at the proliferating number of "networking events" that hold out the promise of meaningful contacts?

Fortunately, there are about 10,000 people eager to assist me—"career coaches"—who, according to the coaching web sites, can help you discover your true occupational "passion," retool your résumé, and hold your hand at every step along the way. The coaches, whose numbers have been doubling every three years, are the core of the "transition industry" that has grown up just since the midnineties, in a perhaps inevitable response to white-collar unemployment.[1] Unlike blue-collar people, the white-collar unemployed are likely to have some assets to invest in their job search; they are, in addition, often lonely and depressed—a perfect market, in other words, for any service promising prosperity and renewed self-esteem. Some coaches have formal training through programs like the Career Coach Academy's fifteen-week course; others are entirely self-anointed. You can declare yourself a coach without any credentials, nor are there any regulatory agencies looking over your shoulder—which means that, for the job seeker, it's the luck of the draw.[2]

I find Morton on the web, listed as a local career coach, although—as I will soon learn—most coaching is done by phone so there is no need for geographic proximity. Morton has been there, is my thought. The background material that

1. See Daniel C. Feldman, "Career Coaching: What HR Professionals Need to Know," *Human Resources Planning* 24:2 (2001), p. 26. Even an improving economy poses no threat to the coaching industry, representatives of the Career Coach Academy and the Career Coach Institute assured me, since companies often hire the same coaches to rev up their executives and employed individuals often seek them out when they see "the handwriting on the wall"— a subject common enough to be the topic of Internet and conference call seminars. Some coaches work as individuals; others are in firms offering, for a fee, office space and equipment for the job seeker.
2. See Stratford Sherman and Alyssa Freas, "The Wild West of Executive Coaching," *Harvard Business Review*, November 2004. Although this article is about executive, as opposed to career, coaching, many individuals do both, and the same lack of credentialing and regulations applies to career coaching generally.

he sends me shows a history of what appear to be high-level, defense-related jobs, including, somewhat datedly, "Senior Intelligence Analyst and Branch Chief Responsible for Analyzing Soviet Military Research." He has given seminars at Carnegie Mellon University and spoken frequently at Kiwanis and Rotary clubs. Surely he can guide my transformation into the marketable middle-level professional I aspire to be. Besides, he assures me, I will not have to pay for our first, trial session.

I have no trouble recognizing him at Starbucks in Charlottesville's Barracks Road Mall; he's the one wearing the "JMU" baseball cap, as promised, a description that encouraged me to come in rumpled gray slacks and sneakers. The top is better, though—black turtleneck, tweed blazer, and pearl earrings—which I am hoping will pass as "business casual." Flustered by being five minutes late because my normal route to the mall was blocked by construction, I stumble over my new name in the handshake phase. He appears not to notice. In fact, he doesn't seem to be much into the noticing business or perhaps already regards me as a disappointment.

After exchanging some observations on the pre-Christmas parking situation at the mall, I lay out my situation for him: I do public relations and event planning, I tell him, but I've been doing it on a freelance basis and am now seeking a stable corporate position with regular benefits, location flexible. How to present myself? Where to begin? I pull out the résumé that I completed over the weekend and slide it across the table toward him. In the worst-case scenario, he will grab it and quiz me on it while holding it in such a way that I will be unable to refresh my memory with an occasional glance. But he regards the stapled papers with only somewhat more enthusiasm than if a fly were advancing across the table toward his arm. Maybe he can tell without reading it, by the very format of the pages—the lack, as I now see it, of bullets and bolding—that it isn't worth a serious coach's attention.

But he is bringing something out of his briefcase—an 8½ × 11 inch transparency—which he places methodically over a sheet of white paper so that I can read: "Core Competencies and Skills," or "the four competencies," as he refers to them. These are Mobilizing Innovation, Managing People and Tasks, Communicating, and Managing Self. This must be what I need—an introduction to the crisp, linear concepts that shape the corporate mind. I am taking notes as fast as I can, but he assures me that he will leave me with copies, so I am free to focus on the content.

The next transparency features a picture of a harness racer and horse, and reads:

Clear mind, skillful driver
Sound spirit, strong horse.
Strong body, sound carriage.
Mind, body, spirit work as one . . .
Path to victory is clear.

The syntax is a bit disturbing, particularly the absence of articles, which gives it a kind of ESL feel, but if modern-day executives can derive management principles from Buddhism or Genghis Khan, as the business sections of bookstores suggest, surely they can imagine themselves as harness racers. The horse, driver, and carriage, Morton is telling me, symbolize Head, Heart, and Gut, but I miss which one is which. This is going to be a lot harder than I anticipated. Already, the four competencies are leaking away from memory, or maybe it should be self-evident that Mobilizing Innovation equals Head or possibly Gut.

With the next transparency, things take a seriously goofy turn. It's titled "Three Centers of Intelligence" and illustrated with characters from *The Wizard of Oz*: the scarecrow, representing "Mental," the tin man, representing "Emotional," and the lion, representing "Instinctual." When he teaches his course on "Spirituality and Business," Morton is explaining, he does this with dolls. That was his wife's idea. She said, "You should have dolls!" and you know what? She went out and found them for him. I profess to being a little sketchy about my *Wizard of Oz*, and Morton digresses into the back story on the tin man, trying to recall how he got such a hard "shell." All I can think is that I'm glad he didn't bring the dolls with him, because Starbucks has gotten crowded now and I wouldn't want it to look like I'm being subjected to some peculiar doll-based form of therapy.

But while I am still struggling to associate the tin man with Emotional and so forth, we move away from Oz to the Enneagram, which is defined in a transparency as:

- A description of personality types
- Based on ancient learning about motivation
- A diagram easily learned and applied
- Provides clues about moving toward balance

The visuals here feature a figure composed of a number of connected triangles enclosed in a circle. I feel a dizziness that cannot be explained by the growing distance from breakfast, and not a single question occurs to me that might shed some light on the ever-deepening complexity before me. Somehow, the Enneagram leads to "The Nine Types," which are also the "nine basic desires or passions." Perhaps sensing my confusion, Morton tells me that, in his course, the Enneagram takes a lot of time to get across. "It's more or less a data dump."

I furrow my brow and nod. All around us, money is being exchanged for muffins in mutually agreeable amounts, and the corporate world continues to function in its usual mindlessly busy, rational way. But the continuance of the corporate enterprise is not something, I realize for the first time, that you can necessarily take for granted. Not if its underlying principles emanate from Oz.

It's a great relief when the higher math of the Enneagram gives way, in the sequence of transparencies, to the familiar *Wizard of Oz* creatures, now seen decorating a series of grids labeled "Emotional Centered Types," "Mentally Centered Types," and "Instinctual Centered Types." On the left side of each grid are five entries, the most intriguing of which is "distorted passion," described by Morton as a "bad passion," or one that you have to recognize and overcome. For example, the lion has as one of its distorted passions "Lust for life. I want to experience and control the entire world," while the scarecrow is potentially burdened with "Avarice—I keep knowledge to myself to avoid being seen as incompetent." I interrupt to ask why keeping knowledge to oneself is called avarice, and he replies evenly, "Because it's keeping something to yourself." Then I notice among the distorted passions, "Gluttony—I can never get enough experience." In among the wanderings of Dorothy in Oz and the "ancient learning" of the Enneagram, Morton—or the inventor of the Enneagram—has managed to weave the Seven Deadly Sins.

What all this leads up to is that I have to take a test, the

Wagner Enneagram Personality Style Scales (WEPSS), which will reveal my personality type and hence what kind of job I should be looking for. I already told Morton what kind of job I'm looking for, but obviously not in a language that fits into his elaborate personal metaphysics. I'll take the test at home, send it to him, and then meet for an evaluation. The whole thing will cost $60.

SO THE SEARCH for a career coach who can actually help me with the mechanics of job searching continues. I register at the CoachLink web site, which nets me three e-mails offering coaching services and one phone call. I go with the phone caller, Kimberly, whose web site describes her as "a career and outplacement consultant, trainer and writer"—for showing initiative—and agree to a weekly half-hour session by phone at $400 a month, or $200 an hour. My "homework," due on our first session, is to "fantasize" about my ideal job. What would my day be like at this ideal job?

It's not a bad assignment. Everyone should take some time for utopian thinking, and what better occasion than when you have nothing else to do? So I fantasize about a small- to medium-size company with offices in a wooded area, mine looking out on a valley and rolling green hills. An espresso cart rolls around every morning and afternoon; there's an on-site gym to which we're encouraged to retreat at least once a day, and the cafeteria features affordable nouvelle cuisine. None of that goes into my written fantasy, however, which focuses on finding a balance between the intense camaraderie of my "team" and periods of creative solitude in my office, which of course has a door—no cubicles for me. I put myself in charge of my team, over which I wield a collegial, "empowering" form of leadership. I am utterly fascinated by my work, whatever it is, and frequently carry on till late at night.

Kimberly, when our first session rolls around, is "excited" by my résumé, "excited" by my fantasy, and generally "excited" to be working with me. I get high marks for the fantasy job: "You're very clear about what you want! Many clients don't get to this stage for months. I think you're going to be a quick study." Already, the excitement level is beginning to exhaust me. In my irritation, I picture her as a short-haired platinum blonde, probably wearing a holiday-themed sweater and looking out from her ranch home on a lawn full of reindeer or gnomes.

As for how she sees herself: "I've gone through some branding processes, and I realize the brand you're getting from me is wildly optimistic, fiercely compassionate, and totally improvisational." I am to think of myself in the same way—as a "brand," or at least a product.

"What do you do in PR?"

I let a beat go by, not sure if this is a test of whether I am actually what I claim to be. But this turns out to be her MO—the teasing question, followed by the dazzlingly insightful answer: "You *sell* things, and now you're going to sell yourself!"

Looking down at my sweatpants and unshod feet, all of which is of course invisible to Kimberly, I mumble about lacking confidence, the tight job market, and the obvious black mark of my age. This last defect elicits a forceful "Be really aware of the negative self-talk you give yourself. Step into the take-charge person you are!"

Now comes the theoretical part. She asks me to think of two overlapping circles. One circle is me, the other is "the world of work," and the overlapping area is "the ideal position for you." "What you need is confidence," Kimberly is saying. "You have to see the glass as half-full, not half-empty." I draw the overlapping circles as she speaks, then redraw them so that they are almost entirely overlapping, thus vastly expanding my employment prospects.

Our half an hour is drawing to a close, I note with relief. She thinks I will need three months of coaching, meaning she will need $1,200. This will be a lot of work for me, she says, because she practices "co-active coaching," which is "very collaborative." "I want you to design me as your best coach," she says, perhaps forgetting that she has already been not only designed but "branded." If I were "designing" her, I'd throw in a major serotonin antagonist to damp down the perkiness, and maybe at some point I will find a tactful way to suggest that she chill. The session has left me drained and her more excited than ever: "We'll dance together here!" is her final promise.

I FEEL THAT I'm not finished with Morton. I should at least take the test so he'll get his $60 and I will perhaps redeem the hour already spent with him. There are 200 questions on the WEPSS test, each in the form of a word or phrase which I am to rate from *A* to *E* in terms of its applicability to me; for example: *dry, pleasure seeking, strength, peacemaker,* and *vengeful.* I sit down at the dining room table with the intention of zipping through the test in ten minutes or less, but it's not as easy as it looks. Am I *special*? From whose vantage point? What about *looking good,* which certainly depends on how much effort has gone into the project? Or *what's the difference*—how can that describe anyone? Most of the terms are adjectives like *judgmental,* but there are plenty of nouns like *fantasy* and even a scattering of verbs like *move against.* Could I describe myself as almost never, occasionally, or almost always *move against*? Am I sometimes, never, or always *wow* or *no big deal*?

Even where the syntax fails to offend me as a writer—or, as I should now put it, a "communications" professional[3]—the answers are by no means obvious. *Harmonious,* for example: sometimes, but it depends on who or what's around to harmonize with. *Avoid conflict*? If possible, but there are times when I seek it out, and in fact enjoy nothing better than, a good table-thumping debate. How about *powerful* or *happy*? I am, I realize, not the kind of person who, well, ever speaks of herself as "not the kind of person who . . ."

The very notion of personality, which is what we are trying to get at here, seems to have very limited application to me and quite possibly everyone else. *Self* is another dodgy concept, since I am, when I subject this "I" to careful inspection, not much more than a swarm of flickering affinities, habits, memories, and predilections that could go either way—toward neediness or independence, for example, courage or cowardice. The best strategy, I decide, is to overcome *hesitant, worrying,* and *correctness seeking* and give what seem like the right, or most admirable, answers. I check "almost always" for *disciplined, high ideals, independent,* and *principled,* while firmly rejecting *lazy, abrasive, procrastinate,* and *laid-back.*

A week later, after Morton has had time to "grade" my personality, we meet at his home to go over the results. It's a mod-

---

3. The corporate disability with language is now an acknowledged problem, with some companies paying for writing courses for their executives. See Sam Dillon, "What Corporate America Cannot Build: A Sentence," *New York Times,* December 7, 2004.

est ranch house in a residential area I have never visited, decorated in a style I recognize as middle-class Catholic, circa
1970—prints of nineteenth-century pastoral scenes, a teddy
bear on a child-size rocking chair, a Madonna overlooking the
armoire. In other words, perfectly normal—at least until we arrive at the dining room table, on which three foot-high dolls
are perched—a scarecrow, a tin man, a lion, and—what movie
is this?—a plastic Elvis.

I decided in advance to lead off with my criticisms of the
test, because if I give them after the results he may think I'm
using them to deflect any criticisms of me that have emerged in
his analysis. How in the world, I ask him, could I say whether
marketing (that's one of the test terms) applies to me? It's a
noun, for heaven's sake, and while I may be "good at marketing," I am not, by any stretch of the imagination, "marketing."
I tell him there's no excuse for such sloppiness, and that I realize that in saying so I may well be revealing something about
my personality: something rigid and unforgiving.

Completely unfazed, Morton picks up the Elvis doll, whose
legs are sticking out at a right angle to his trunk in some
hideous form of rigor mortis, and tells me that he uses it to
make the point that "there is about as much similarity between
the doll and the real Elvis as there is between you and your
personality type." I want to object that the doll does resemble
the real Elvis, in his youth anyway and before his unfortunate
weight gain; at least anyone could see that it is not a Barbara
doll. But that misses the larger questions of what I am doing
here if the test is meaningless and what it has to do with finding a job anyway. Besides, he's putting Elvis down on a side
table now, leaving us alone with the Oz crew.

We move on to the results. It turns out that my scores

"could fit almost any personality type." I'm highest in Original and Effective, and when you plot that out on an Enneagram, the diagonal lines connect me to Good and Loving. This makes me a tin man with a little lion thrown in, he says, fingering the appropriate dolls. Next, he brings out the baffling transparencies, which have been sitting here all along in a file folder. This time I resolve to get to the bottom of things, but when he flashes the transparency labeled "The Enneagram Symbol," with its nested triangles, all I can come up with is, "What is the circle doing here?" It's there, he explains, "for graphic unity"—meaning that he just likes the look of it?—and also to show that "we are talking about a whole person." And the big triangle? I continue, losing heart. "Those are the three centers of intelligence."

It turns out, though, that my Original, Effective, Good and Loving traits are not the point. The point is to understand my "nonresourceful" side, which seems to be my bad side, because this is what I need to do something about. Some people, Morton says, addressing the brown and wintry lawn outside the dining room window, resist hearing about this side. One woman, a schoolteacher, broke into tears when she learned about hers. In my case, the nonresourceful side includes being overly sensitive and prone to melancholy and envy, not to mention the bad traits that come up when you draw diagonals from Loving and Effective. What this comes down to, in a practical sense, is that, given my highly emotional and artistic personality (where did *that* come from?), I probably "don't write very well." The "suggested activity," in my case, would be "intensive journaling workshops" to polish my writing skills.

There is nothing to do but mumble my thanks, write out the check, and leave. I think of my father, whose personality traits included brash, cynical, bombastic, obnoxious, charming, kindly, and falling-down drunk, yet who managed to rise from the copper mines of Butte to the corporate stratosphere, ending up as vice president of research for a multinational firm. Did he ever take a personality test or submit to executive coaching? Or were things different in the fifties and sixties, with a greater emphasis on what you could actually *do*? What would he have made of Morton, the dolls, and the ancient wisdom of the Enneagram? I drive home with his deep guffaws echoing in my head.

MORTON DOES HAVE one useful tip to offer: if I want help with my résumé, I should see Joanne, whose e-mail address he will e-mail me. Joanne turns out to be available at the same fee as Kimberly, and meets me at a coffeehouse only ten minutes from home—not the ideal venue since I've been to it before and there is a remote chance of encountering someone who knows me. I am expecting an impeccably dressed southern-lady type, not the rumpled, makeup-free, fiftyish woman who greets me. She's done "development" in the nonprofit world, she tells me, but has shifted—she says nothing about the circumstances prompting the shift—into executive coaching and is just coming from "a strategic planning meeting at Pepsi." I bond at once; she is the anti-Kimberly, noninvasive and utterly down-to-earth. Although I'm not sure whether their functions overlap, I decide it's best not to tell Joanne about Kimberly or vice versa.

Of my three coaches so far, Joanne is the first to give me some real reason for hope. She picks up on the word *speech-writing* buried in my first, feeble attempt at a résumé, and tells me to ramp it up as a salable skill, and I realize, yes, that's something I can actually do. Up to this point, crisscrossing my contempt for Morton and Kimberly's psychobabble, has been a deep strain of anxiety that I may, in fact, have nothing to offer, no skills of any relevance to the wide world of moneymaking. My PR and event-planning experience is, after all, derived from the more easygoing end of the nonprofit world and may not fully apply to the corporate setting. But speechwriting is speechwriting—from the initial joke or anecdote, through the marshaling of facts, to the exhortatory finale—and I've been doing it for decades. What no one needs to know is that all the speeches I've written were delivered by myself.

Joanne has other useful advice: Take *I* and *my* (as in "my responsibilities included . . .") out of the résumé, which, I'm beginning to see, should have an odd, disembodied tone, as if my life had been lived by some invisible Other. Break everything I claim to have done down into its smaller, constituent, activities, so that, for example, I didn't just "plan" an event, I "met with board to develop objectives" and went on through the various other phases of the job to "facilitate post-event evaluations." What can I say? It certainly fills up space. And then her most ingenious tip of all: go to the professional association web sites for my putative professions and pick up the buzzwords, or professional lingo. If she doesn't know I'm a complete fake, and I don't think I've given her any reason to suspect that I am, she nonetheless has a remarkably clear idea of how to perpetrate the fakery. Which may just be the essence of résumé writing.

I am not, of course, pinning all hopes on my coaches. For one thing, I have been fleshing out my new identity: opening a checking account for Barbara Alexander, ordering her a credit card, having business cards made up for her at Kinko's. She already, of course, has an e-mail address. As for clothes, she will have to share mine, and at this point I am still clueless enough to imagine that the outfits I use for lecturing on college campuses will pass muster in the business world. I expunge *Ehrenreich* from the greetings on my home and cell phones; I buy new glasses frames, striking dark ones, chosen solely for their difference from my ordinary dull ones. I start cruising the business section of the local Barnes and Noble.

Besides, I have already learned from Kimberly the necessity of being "proactive" and also a "self-starter." My résumé is too much of a work in progress to warrant posting on the major Internet job search sites like Monster and HotJobs, but there's still no end of things to do on the web. I go to the event planners' professional association web site and pilfer it for event-planning jargon to pad out my résumé. Way beyond just planning events, I expand into "providing on-site management" and "evaluating return on investment."

Looking for advice and, better yet, company, I Google all possible combinations of *unemployed, white-collar, professional,* and *jobs.* These are not the best keywords, I discover. First, jobless white-collar people are not "unemployed"; they are "in transition" or perhaps engaged in a "job search." Only the lowly—the blue- and pink-collar people—admit to actual "unemployment." Second, avoid the word *job,* which, unless carefully modified, will lead to numerous sites in which it is prefaced by *hand* or *blow.*

The time I spend on the web has a dank and claustrophobic feel. After traversing a few links, I forget where I started and am lost among the pages full of advice, support groups, networking events, and coaching opportunities geared to various

salary levels. I join something called ExecuNet for a fee of
$150 and decide that's what I am—an executive. I throw *exec-
utive* in among my keywords and start up the searches again,
leading to still more support groups, networking events, and so
forth. Is this a total waste of time, job-search-wise? I might as
well be hacking through thick jungle undergrowth with a
bread knife instead of a machete.

At my second session with Joanne, conducted by phone,
Barbara Alexander begins to earn my respect. I had initially
thought of her as a stay-at-home wife who didn't have to work
for the money—just enjoyed her little dabblings in PR and
event planning, sort of as an extension of her busy social life.
Her husband must have been pretty well-heeled, and I suspect
that his contacts provided her with most of her clients. Divorce has confronted her with the need to earn money, an enterprise for which she is sorely unprepared. But now Joanne
asks me what has distinguished my work from that of other PR
and event-planning people. I search for an answer and come
up with: "My thorough research on whatever topic or theme
I'm working on . . . My goal is to be thoroughly conversant
with the major issues and trends in the field, to the point where
I can participate in substantive decision making, like picking a
keynote speaker."

"*Conversant!*" Joanne exclaims in a rare show of enthusiasm, "I love that word! We'll use it in the résumé or maybe the
cover letter." So Barbara Alexander is not an airhead at all but
a towering intellectual of the event-planning field.

Meanwhile I have homework from Kimberly. First I have to
fill in the questionnaire she included in my "Client Discovery
Packet," asking me, among other things, to list five adjectives
that describe me at my best and five that describe me at my

worst. For the best I choose *energetic, focused, intelligent, compassionate,* and *creative,* while for my dark side I choose *anxious, compulsive, disorganized, distractible,* and *depressed*—all true at various times except for distractible, which was simply a way of filling in space.

What are my three major fears? I offer "too old to find work" and "likely to end up in poverty," but cannot think of a third. The only question that gives me pause is "list five things you are tolerating or putting up with in your life at present (examples: disorganized office, disrespectful relationships, poor communication, etc.)." That's it: disorganized office. Stacks of paper mount and subside around in me in waves; the floor moonlights as a filing space; empty cups and glasses crowd the desk, along with unpaid bills, unanswered letters, manuscripts I am supposed to review. Talk about a "distorted passion," as Morton would put it; to judge from my home office, I have the administrative talents of a twelve-year-old boy. Kimberly had promised in our initial talk that I would come out of our co-active process not only with a job but with "a whole new view of myself." With luck, the new view will be far less cluttered.

The other Kimberly assignment is to take yet another personality test, the Myers-Briggs Type Indicator, which is marginally craftier than the WEPSS, in that I am not asked simply to choose the attributes that fit me, but am given somewhat more roundabout questions, such as "Do you usually get along better with (A) imaginative people, or (B) realistic people?" Once again, the only sensible approach is a random one. Do I usually show my feelings freely or keep my feelings to myself? Hmm, depends on how socially acceptable those feelings might be. If it's a desire to inflict grievous bodily harm on some person currently in my presence—well, no. When I go somewhere for the day, would I rather plan what I will do and when, or "just go"? Again, it's somewhat different for a court appearance than for a trip to the mall. I race through the test with the mad determination of a monkey that's been given a typewriter and assigned to generate Shakespeare's oeuvre, hoping that some passably coherent individual emerges.

CAREER COACHES CAN perhaps be forgiven for using baseless personality tests to add a veneer of scientific respectability to the coaching process. But the tests enjoy wide credibility, not just among coaches but among corporate decision makers. In 1993, the Myers-Briggs test was administered to three million Americans; eighty-nine of the Fortune top 100 companies use it to help slot their white-collar employees into the appropriate places in the hierarchy.[4] On its web site, the Enneagram Institute lists, among the companies supposedly using the Enneagram test to sort out their employees, Amoco, AT&T, Avon, Boeing, DuPont, eBay, General Mills, General Motors, Alitalia Airlines, KLM Airlines, Hewlett-Packard, Toyota, Procter & Gamble, International Weight Watchers, Reebok Health Clubs, Motorola, Prudential Insurance, and Sony. Amazon offers a score of books on the Enneagram, none of them apparently critical, including *The Enneagram in Love and Work, The Spiritual Dimension of the Enneagram,* and *The Enneagram for Managers.*

It is true that I encountered the Enneagram in the particu-

4. Annie Murphy Paul, *The Cult of Personality: How Personality Tests Are Leading Us to Miseducate Our Children, Mismanage Our Companies, and Misunderstand Ourselves* (New York: Free Press, 2004), p. 125.

larly wacky company of *The Wizard of Oz*. But the test I took was the real thing, which, a web search reveals, is variously said to be derived from Sufism, Buddhism, Jesuit philosophy, and Celtic lore—with a generous undergirding of numerology. The early twentieth-century Russian mystic G. I. Gurdjieff seems to have been a fount of inspiration, but the actual development of the Enneagram theory is usually credited to two men— Oscar Ichazo, a Bolivian-born mystic, and Claudio Naranjo, a psychiatrist who made his mark in the nineteen sixties by employing hallucinogenic drugs in psychotherapy. Whatever "ancient learning" the Enneagram test purports to represent, it is nothing more than a pastiche of wispy New Age yearnings for some mystic unity underlying the disorder of human experience.

Even the more superficially rational of these tests, the Myers-Briggs Type Indicator, possesses not a shred of scientific respectability according to Annie Murphy Paul's 2004 book, *The Cult of Personality*. It was devised, in the early forties, by a layperson—a homemaker in fact—who had become fascinated by her son-in-law's practical, detailed-oriented personality, which was so different from her own, more intuitive, approach. Inspired by the psychoanalyst Carl Jung's notion of "types"—which were by no means meant to be innate or immutable—Katharine Briggs devised a test to sort humanity into sixteen distinct types, all of them fortunately benign. (There were no psychopaths, of the kind who might show up at work one day with an automatic weapon, in Briggs's universe.) To her eternal frustration, the test never won respect from the academic psychology profession, and not only because of her outsider status. Serious psychologists have never been convinced that people can be so readily sorted into "types."

Leaving aside the validity of "types," the Myers-Briggs Type Indicator has zero predictive value even in its own terms. In one study, undertaken by proponents of Myers-Briggs, only 47 percent of people tested fell into the same category on a second administration of the test. Another study found 39 to 76 percent of those tested assigned to a different "type" upon retesting weeks or years later. Some people's "types" have been found to vary according to the time of day. Paul concludes that "there is no evidence that [Briggs's] sixteen distinct types have any more validity than the twelve signs of the zodiac."[5]

So why is the corporate world, which we think of as so fixated on empirical, in fact, quantifiable, measures of achievement like the "bottom line," so attached to these meaningless personality tests? One attraction must be that the tests lend a superficial rationality to the matching of people with jobs. No one, after all, wants a sadistic personnel director or a morbidly shy publicist; and if you failed at one job, it is probably comforting to be told that it was simply not a good "fit" for your inner nature. As Paul writes:

> The administration of personality tests is frequently presented as a gesture of corporate goodwill, a generous acknowledgement of employees' uniqueness. Under this banner of respect for individuality, organizations are able to shift responsibility for employee satisfaction onto that obligatory culprit, "fit." There's no bad worker and no bad workplace, only a bad fit between the two.[6]

5. Paul, *Cult of Personality,* pp. 133–34.
6. Ibid., p. 130.

Of course, if the function of the tests is really ideological—to promote the peg-in-hole theory of employment—they do not have to be in any way accurate as predictors of performance or satisfaction. They serve more as underpinnings of corporate etiquette, allowing employers to rationalize rejection or dismissal in terms of an inadequate "fit." We believe that there is a unique slot for each person, the tests announce—even though we may fail to find it in your particular case.

My job, though, is to find a "fit," however wobbly, in any institutional structure that will have me. And with this simple task in mind, the personality tests seem even more mysterious. If I am a public relations person by training and experience, what good will it do me to discover that my personality is better suited to a career as an embalmer? Presumably there are extroverted engineers and introverted realtors, who nevertheless manage to get the job done. The peculiar emphasis on "personality," as opposed to experience and skills, looms like a red flag, but I have no way of knowing yet what the warning's about.

MY LONG-THREATENED one-hour make-up session with Kimberly finally arrives, and the reason for this ghastly intrusion into my time is that I blew off a prior scheduled session out of sheer sullenness and inability to simulate the cheerfulness that a successful Kimberly interaction requires. We start with the results of the Myers-Briggs test. "You're an ENTJ," she announces. "I was so excited when I saw it!"

"Remember the two overlapping circles?" she quizzes me. I acknowledge that I do. One was the world, one was me.

"Well," she explains, "the personality is part of *you.*"

"As opposed to the world?"

"Yes! Each letter signifies something, and together you get a kind of fruit salad! The *E*—that's for *extrovert.* You know that word?"

"Mmm."

"It means that you get your energy external to yourself." She too is an *E,* and being *E* is "good news for the job search, because introverts have a lot of trouble getting out there."

I cannot think of how to respond, which seems to occasion a rare moment of self-doubt in Kimberly. "Do you agree about the *E* part?" she asks. "Do you feel drained by spending time with people? Or energized?"

In this case, definitely drained, but I am loath to disown the good news of my *E*-ness. She proceeds through the letters, pausing in between to let me acknowledge the truth of them. "*N* is for *intuitive*, as opposed to *S*, which is a kind of detail person. The challenge, for an *N*, is that they are kind of disorganized." Ah yes, that's me. *T* is for "thinker as opposed to feeling," which is very good although she herself tests on the feeling side, and *J* means I like "closure on things." The danger there is that I might come to "premature closure," and she can help me slow down a little. I suspect this is a veiled reference to my recent insistence on a time frame for our coaching process, or at least some estimate of when I would be released into the world as a viable candidate—a demand she had weaseled out of.

"Now for the really good news," she tells me. "ENTJ is also called the *commandant*. They usually rise to the highest level in organizations. You are a natural leader!"

"So I should apply for CEO jobs?"

"Well no, but you can tell people you have really strong leadership qualities. Would you be comfortable with that?"

I tell her I'm not sure and, ever so tactfully, that I don't really see the point of this. Never mind that the ENTJ version of me bears no resemblance to the emotional, artistic, melancholy, and envious neurotic revealed by Morton's WEPSS test, which of course goes unmentioned here.

"The point is," she interjects, "that it gives you *language!*" She directs me to open the booklet that she had sent me along with the test, *Introduction to Type in Organizations*, second edition. After some scuffling with the detritus on my desk, I find it and turn to page 31, as instructed. There I find a list of the organizational qualities of ENTJs, including "take charge quickly," "develop well-thought-out plans," and "run as much of the organization as possible." "So?" I ask.

"You can say it in your résumé!" she responds, and I begin to detect just the slightest impatience with me.

I tell her I can't say I develop well-thought-out plans just because this test says I do, and we toss that one around for a few minutes, with her insisting it's who I *am*. "Well, I don't think I can walk into some new situation and announce that I can take charge or that I'm a natural leader."

"Why not?"

"Because it sounds boastful."

And now she can no longer suppress the irritation, answering only with a mocking "Helloo-oo-oo?"

Unless I can fake a bomb attack on my home, we have twenty-five minutes to go, which I would rather not spend being bullied into "owning," as she puts it, my inner commandant. I have a question prepared. Over our several sessions so far, I have intuited that she wants me to be more like her—

upbeat, cheery, "in the moment," and excruciatingly overreactive. In my web searches, I have come across several enjoinders to, in fact, become more Kimberly-like if I intend to land a job. One such site, called Professionals in Transition, features an article on developing a "winning attitude," which advises that

> your personal attitude will determine the ultimate success of your job campaign. If you are angry with your former employer, or have a negative attitude, it will show. Studies have shown that the hiring process is over 90% emotional. In other words, if I like you, I may hire you. If you are perceived as being hostile, negative or carrying significant emotional baggage, it will send a mixed message that can significantly hinder your job campaign efforts.

The idea that hiring decisions are "90% emotional" is deeply discouraging. What happened to skills and achievements? But if a winning attitude is what I need, I am determined to develop one, so I ask Kimberly how to go about this.

Maybe it's hard for her to imagine not having one, because she immediately wants to know what stands in my way. "Like what are you worried about?"

"My age, for one thing."

"So the trick is to make your age a nonissue. What age would you like to be?"

I tell her I'm fine with my current age, but clearly it doesn't meet her standards. She goes off into an explanation of the difference between "biological" and "chronological" age, and will not be budged by my insistence that I am happy to be who I am, thank you. "Wouldn't you say you *feel* like thirty-seven?"

Actually, I feel much better than I did at thirty-seven, but, what the hell, I agree to go along with her idée fixe that thirty-seven is my "biological age."

"SO? Then you ARE thirty-seven!" she announces triumphantly.

"But you can figure out my age from my résumé, which lists the year of my college graduation."

"*Absolutely* don't put your graduation date on your résumé," she advises, "and eliminate all the earlier jobs. It shouldn't go back more than ten years, fifteen max."

This takes my breath away. She might as well have instructed me to amputate my legs at the knees. I mourn for Barbara Alexander, who had been fluffing up so nicely and now must be contracted into a thirty-seven-year-old midget. It has to be done, though; all references to a life prior to 1989 must be expunged from my résumé.

Even more staggering is my other major "takeaway" from this session (I'm at least picking up some jargon): that I am not the only phony in the job-searching business. What I've been learning from Kimberly and to a certain extent also from the stolid Joanne is how to lie—how to plump up an undistinguished résumé, how to project a kind of confidence I neither feel nor deserve to feel. Deception is part of the game. Even getting along with Kimberly, which I admit I haven't done very well—she once utilized the "dance" metaphor to tell me, "We're dancing, but we're stepping all over each other's toes"—has been part of the training process. I can be what I want to be, is the message, so long as I act like I believe it. I am ready, or almost ready, to press on out into the world.

two

Stepping Out into the World of Networking

All the web-site advice I have gleaned about job searching emphasizes the importance of "networking." At first, in my innocence, I had envisioned this as a freewheeling exercise in human sociability, possibly involving white wine. Joanne and Kimberly, though, have impressed on me that networking takes hard work, discipline, and perseverance. When I informed Kimberly of my intention to launch the networking phase, she caught me up short with a demand to hear my "elevator speech." This, it turns out, is a thirty- to forty-five-second self-advertisement, which in my case, Kimberly suggests, should begin with "Hi, I'm Barbara Alexander, and I'm a crackerjack PR person!" In one of our phone sessions, Joanne shared with me her own elevator speech—it turns out that she too is job searching—and when I ventured that it sounded a bit stiff, she confessed to not having fully memorized it yet.

Hours of Internet searching have netted me a "networking

event" only two and a half hours away at the Forty-Plus Club of Washington, D.C. Founded to help middle-aged executive job seekers during the Depression, the club attracted to its first advisory board such corporate and cultural luminaries as Tom Watson, the founder of IBM; James Cash Penney, of JC Penney; Arthur Godfrey, the TV personality; and Norman Vincent Peale, the author of *The Power of Positive Thinking*—whom I take to be the intellectual granddad of Kimberly. Despite their establishment origins, the nineteen Forty-Plus Clubs around the nation are the closest thing one can find to a grassroots organization of the white-collar unemployed. The clubs are run entirely by volunteers, conveniently drawn from the pool of unemployed, middle-aged, white-collar people.

The event starts at 9:30 on a rainy January morning, at an impressive address near Dupont Circle, although the actual space turns out to be a dark, almost belligerently undecorated basement suite. Pamela, who's about fifty and dressed in a long, close-fitting skirt that creates a definite mermaid effect, greets me in the corridor and directs me to a table where Ted, also about fifty, is presiding over the name tag distribution. He wears a wrinkled suit and tie, set off, intriguingly, by a black eye. No, he instructs, I am not to take a red name tag; as a "new person," I am assigned to blue. Looking off to the side a little, perhaps to draw attention from his eye, he confides that the networking will proceed until 10:00, at which time we will be treated to a lecture on "New Year's resolutions for job searchers."

Time is short, so I get right down to work, going up to my fellow job seekers, introducing myself, and asking what kinds of jobs they're looking for. About fifteen people have drifted in so far and distributed themselves among the chairs arranged in semicircles around a podium. All are middle-aged white guys, and I manage to successfully connect with several of them before the seats fill up, hampering my efforts to circulate: Mike, who's in finance; Jim, who is also in PR and, alarmingly enough, has been looking for seven months. A man who identifies himself as a media manager latches onto me next, relating that he is bitter—his word—because he gave eleven years to Time Warner and has just been laid off in some inexplicable corporate reorganization, leaving him with two teenagers to feed and educate. So these are my people, my new constituency—men, and now a few women, who will go home as I will to a desk off the dining room and an afternoon of lonely web searching.

I had worried about not having an elevator speech prepared but none of the people I talk to offers one, much less asks to hear mine. What were Kimberly and Joanne thinking of? Most of the job searchers present wear expressions of passivity and mild expectation; clothing-wise, few have advanced much beyond the sweatpants level. Going by such superficials alone, I'd be surprised if there's another ENTJ in the bunch. In fact, even as the place fills up with a total of about thirty people, all in the same white and over-the-hill demographic, I notice that I'm the only one systematically working the room. One of the later arrivals, Michael, barely responds to my smiling overtures, burying his head in the *Washington Post*. From him I move on to Frank, a rumpled-looking fellow of about sixty, who says he is a consultant in financial matters.

"Do you know what's wrong with Bush?" he asks me. "He's never had to work; he's had everything handed to him on a silver platter."

When I nod in agreement and say that I am also

consulting—a term I've learned to substitute for *freelancing*—
he observes that "that's what they want us all to be—
consultants." Because then they can use us when they need us
and get rid of us when they don't—no benefits or other entan-
glements involved.

At 10:00 the meeting is opened by Merle, who explains that
the "core program" of the Forty-Plus Club is a three-week
"boot camp" aimed at turning newbies like myself into mean,
lean, job-searching machines. I find myself slavishly cathected
to Merle; she is beautiful, for one thing, about my age or a little younger, and awesomely poised. I take her to be my female
executive template—kindly in tone but brooking no devia-
tions from the business at hand. She says she's been job searching for nine months—which, given the setting, must be meant
as a qualification for her leadership role—but the information
is definitely disturbing. If such a paragon of executive virtue
can go jobless for almost a year, what hope is there for someone in my situation?

Merle introduces our guest speaker, Joe Loughran, a former
"Wall Street Associate" who has a Harvard MBA and now
runs his own business as a career coach, or "transition acceler-
ant" as the brief biography on the Forty-Plus web site puts it.
A large, mild-mannered fellow turned out preppily in khakis
and red sweater, he begins with a bit of self-deprecation on the
theme of giving up chocolate as a New Year's resolution—he
"would have trouble with that"—and then seems to have trouble relinquishing the chocolate theme, getting tangled up in
how resolutions can have a "domino effect": you don't buy a
new suit because you're waiting to lose a few pounds from the
chocolate deprivation, and then, because you don't have a new

suit, you don't go for an important interview. The lesson would seem to be: don't bother with resolutions; lecture over.

But things pick up when he asks us what obstacles we face in our job searches. A half-dozen hands go up, offering such obstacles as fear, inertia, embarrassment, procrastination, money, "nonlinear career path," and the mysterious challenge of "staying up." I catch Ted, who is standing against the wall, nodding vigorously at each of the obstacles, suggesting that he knows each of them all too well. Joe is doing his best to keep up on a flip chart. I throw in that I get overwhelmed by all the things there are to do, lack priorities. This is recorded as "scheduling."

At this point I am expecting some solutions from Joe, but Merle, who has never abdicated her position at the front of the room, steps forward to ask, "What have some people done to manage?" I want *Joe's* job is what I am thinking, which seems to involve no more than note taking and serving, in his brilliant red sweater, as a human stoplight. But solutions to my problem of "scheduling" are pouring in as fast as I can write them down. "I make a daily schedule including Internet searches and exercise," one woman contributes. "This forces me to be accountable even if I'm the only one in the room, managing myself." Someone else adds, "I set the alarm for the same time I did when I was working. I get up, shave, dress, just as if I was going to work." Another solution: enroll your spouse as a "supervisor," to remind you "you said you were going to do such and such today."

This advice comes as a surprise: job searching is not joblessness; it is a job in itself and should be structured to resemble one, right down to the more regrettable features of employment, like having to follow orders—orders which are in this case self-generated. Something about this scenario carries a whiff of necrophilia. I think of the fabled resident of old Key West who somehow had his beloved's corpse preserved in a condition congenial to continued physical intimacies for years after her death. So, too, we are not to accept joblessness but to hold on desperately to some faint simulacrum of employment.

Everyone agrees on the necessity of managing oneself much as a real boss might, although this presents immediate conceptual problems: if "selling myself" had seemed like a tricky form of self-objectification, "managing myself" takes the process even farther, into the realm of mental cloning. I picture the Barbaras splitting off into worker-Barbara (the one who sits at the computer and searches for jobs), product-Barbara (the one who has to be "sold"), and now manager-Barbara (whose responsibility is to oversee the other two)—all contending for dominance in the same cramped office space. I recall that one of the mysterious "Core Competencies" in the scheme developed by Morton, my first coach, had indeed been "Managing Self."

But the theme here, I am beginning to see, is pain management and structured grieving. If you have been spat out by the great corporate machine and left to contemplate your presumed inadequacy, it makes sense to fill the day with micro-tasks, preferably supervised by someone else. Imagining one's search as a "job" must satisfy the Calvinist craving to be doing something, anything, of a worklike nature, and Americans may be especially prone to Calvinist angst. We often credit some activity with the phrase "at least it keeps me busy"—as if busyness were a desirable state regardless of how you achieve it. As I later learn in Harvey Mackay's business best seller *We Got*

Fired! . . . And It's the Best Thing That Ever Happened to Us, job searching, properly undertaken, should be far more time-consuming than an actual job: "If you have a job, then you might have the luxury of working 9:00 to 5:00. If you're getting a job, then plan on twelve to sixteen hours a day."[1]

The alternative to manufactured busyness is flat-out depression, as a large gray-haired man seems to confirm when, in an apparent non sequitur, he raises his hand to caution that "introspection can be very powerful if you do it in the right frame of mind. Otherwise it can get you down." One wonders what dark nights of the soul he has endured in the course of his search, but for Merle and Joe, his comment serves only as a segue to "staying up," which amounts to maintaining a winning attitude, even in the face of despair. Here the grim Calvinism of self-management suddenly gives way to a wan hedonism: We should go to the gym, networking with other gym-goers while we're there. Have lunch with a friend. Make a list of things you enjoy. The dark-haired, somewhat exotic-looking woman sitting next to me, who has been looking for a communications job for six months, leans over and whispers naughtily, "I take antidepressants. Do you think I should shout that out?" We both giggle, although it isn't really all that funny.

We are on to "Fear" and Joe asks what we are afraid of. "Failure" comes up in various forms, and I add "rejection." There's no dodging fear. Joe exhorts us to "get in its face," and a woman, who I later learn is a career coach herself, stresses the need "to really feel your fear." This seems to delight Pamela, who has remained standing, like Merle, though off to the side: "That's honoring your feelings!" But fear, once faced,

1. Mackay, *We Got Fired!*, p. 56.

is quickly abolished. As Joe summarizes the topic, "The point is, what is there to be afraid of? It's Nike. Just do it."

Now Pamela has an idea: laughter, specifically, "artificial laughter." At least you start with artificial laughter, which can magically evolve into the real thing. She produces a five-second-long laugh, followed by "See?" But the fake laugh fails to catch on; most people are looking at her with slight alarm. She tries again in a higher register—Ha ha ha ha ha, Ha ha ha ha ha—and out of solidarity I try to join in. Otherwise, though, there is an appalled silence.

We move on through Health and Money to an obstacle Joe calls "the Gap" and identifies as a chronological defect in one's résumé—caused, for example, by a spell of unemployment. This may be a measure of my extreme naïveté and longstanding distance from the world of regular employment, but I had not realized that being unemployed may in and of itself disqualify one for a job.[2] Joe wants us to acknowledge the Gap, accept it, and emphasize the bright side of it, such as what we learned while enduring it. I raise my hand and ask, "What if the Gap was homemaking?" I'm expecting at least some nods of commiseration from the women in the room, but I might as well have announced that I've devoted a chunk of my career to collecting welfare. Joe looks away uncomfortably, forcing Merle to step forward and promise that this subject will be dealt with "in boot camp." Ted, from his position near the

---

2. A period of unemployment is also likely to damage one's credit rating. In a fiendish catch-22, 35 percent of U.S. companies now run a credit check as a condition for employment, up from 19 percent in 1996—making it far more difficult to bounce back after hard times. See Marie Szaniszlo, "Employers Turning to a New Kind of Ref Check," *Boston Herald,* December 12, 2004.

wall, speaks up to suggest that I stress "the time management skills you developed while managing children."

Yeah, right, like I'm going to have résumé entries like "negotiated complex preteen transportation issues" and "provided in-home leadership to highly creative team of three"? I think of all the recent articles about upper-middle-class, professional mothers who opt to stay home with their children during the early years, fully expecting to pick up their careers at full stride later on. One of the Gen-X moms interviewed in a *Time* article "desperately hopes that she won't be penalized for her years at home."[3] But the Mommy Track appears to end right here, in a support group for the long-term unemployed.

At precisely 11:00, Joe winds up to hearty applause, and I choose this break to start edging toward the door. I have just reached it when Merle, who is now presiding over a little ritual honoring a boot-camp graduate who has actually found a job, calls out, "Barbara, it's not time to go yet!" Stunned that she can read my name tag at this distance and mortified to have been singled out, I stand there and watch as a fortysomething Asian-American—he is today's lucky job finder—takes a mallet and hits a large metal bell, making him a "bell ringer." I take a step backward through the door frame, but Pamela is directly behind me, blocking the way. "You're losing your name tag," she whispers to me. I smooth it down obligingly, if only because I am beginning to lose confidence in the physical possibility of egress. If I were to take another step toward freedom, I might get jumped by some of the beefier cult members.

Because that's how it's beginning to look to me. If profit is

3. Claudia Wallis, "The Case for Staying Home," *Time,* March 22, 2004.

not the aim, and it can't be, since everyone in charge is a volunteer, then what could it matter if one potential recruit leaks away after the formal proceedings? I get the paranoid sense that I have fallen into the Cult of Merle, and what happens next only seems to confirm this. New people like myself— there are only six of us—are to repair into a side room for a special session of their own, suggesting that the reason for Pamela's concern about my name tag had to do with the ease of sorting out who is new.

The special gathering for new people turns out to be a heavy sell for the boot camp, which costs close to $600 for three weeks of eight-hour days. Ted and Pamela officiate, beginning with some videotaped testimonies to the effectiveness of the boot camp, while we new people sit in frozen expectation. It will be an intense experience, Ted advises, ranging from résumé development to body language and elevator speeches. Among other things, we will each star in a three-minute videotape sales pitch for ourselves, which will be revised until perfect. He is standing next to where I am sitting, going over a poster describing the boot camp's syllabus, when suddenly he bursts into tears.

My mind had wandered during his presentation, so I have to do a quick rewind to recall the emotional subtext of what he had been saying at the moment of breakdown—something about a neighbor of his who had been laid off and not said anything to Ted about it for months. A broken friendship? Or just a reminder to him of how lonely the first months of unemployment were? And how did he get the black eye anyway?

I have to restrain myself from reaching out and putting my hand on his arm, but Pamela is impatiently insisting that she take over the poster presentation. Thus rebuked, Ted struggles and pulls himself together, although the tears are still running down his cheeks.

I finally get up to leave, resigned to never knowing what was up with Ted or whether Merle, our charismatic leader, is a saint or a demon. No doubt there's nothing cultish going on, and the only reason the volunteers push the boot camp so insistently is that it gives them something to do: better to immerse yourself in Forty-Plus activities than to sit home alone waiting for the phone to ring. But Ted's breakdown does reinforce the impression that, whatever is going on in the corporate world today, whatever wild process is chewing up men and women and spitting them out late in life, damage is definitely done.

AT MY NEXT session with Kimberly, I report that I've been successfully networking. "So did you make some contacts?" she wants to know.

"Just the people I networked with," I admit, explaining the context of the Forty-Plus Club.

"But they're unemployed! There's no point to networking with unemployed people unless they have contacts in companies you want to work for!"

So much for my people, then, the great army of the white-collar unemployed. They're not worth the time of day. You are encouraged to go to networking events, only to be told that you've been wasting your time.

"Look," she says, trying a new tack. "What companies *do* you want to work for?"

I've had a new insight into this, so I tell her, "I've been thinking . . . I've done a lot in the health field, maybe I should emphasize that more. Maybe like a drug company."

"A drug company—good! And what else?"

"A medical supply company?"

"And what else?"

"Uh, I don't know."

"A hospital! What about a hospital?"

I have to admit that I didn't know or had forgotten that hospitals maintain PR staffs—another reason for resentment when perusing the medical bills. So how would I network with hospital people?

"You have a doctor, don't you?"

I acknowledge that I do.

"So network with him!"

"But she barely has time to tell me my blood pressure, much less talk about my career."

"Does she have a receptionist?"

I acknowledge this too.

"So network with her!"

I don't tell her, and I'm not proud of this, but I find the suggestion insulting. Here I am, a "seasoned professional" according to my résumé, and I'm supposed to be pestering the clinic receptionist for job leads? Not to mention the fact that the receptionist appears to be even more distracted and rushed than the doctor. Meanwhile, Kimberly is going on about the need to network *everywhere,* like with the person I'm sitting next to on a plane. Almost anyone seems to be worth my smiling attentions except my brothers and sisters in the job-searching business.

Session over, I refill my iced tea and sit down to reflect on my aversion to Kimberly, which seems completely out of proportion to the circumstances. I hired her; she was my choice; she's supposed to be helping me. Beyond that, of course, this is only a journalistic venture anyway, in which I have no real-life emotional stake. Yet the dislike is reaching hatelike dimensions, and it seems to me that if I could get to the bottom of it, I would be a leg up on the whole job-search process. She represents something about the corporate world that repels me, some deep coldness masked as relentless cheerfulness. In fact the "mask" theme has come up several times in my background reading. Richard Sennett, for example, in *The Corrosion of Character: The Personal Consequences of Work in the New Capitalism*, and Robert Jackall, in *Moral Mazes: The World of Corporate Managers*, refer repeatedly to the "masks" that corporate functionaries are required to wear, like actors in an ancient Greek drama. According to Jackall, corporate managers stress the need to exercise iron self-control and to mask all emotion and intention behind bland, smiling, and agreeable public faces.[4]

Kimberly seems to have perfected the requisite phoniness, and even as I dislike her, my whole aim is to be welcomed into the same corporate culture that she seems to have mastered, meaning that I need to "get in the face" of my revulsion and overcome it. But until I reach that transcendent point, I seem to be stuck in an emotional space left over from my midteen years: I hate you; please love me.

ALL RIGHT, DISTASTEFUL as the idea may be, I do have to structure my job search in some joblike fashion. I determine that my daily plan will be as follows:

---

4. Robert Jackall, *Moral Mazes: The World of Corporate Managers* (New York: Oxford University Press, 1988), p. 47.

7:30 A.M.: Get up, eat breakfast, read the paper, check CNN for major disasters—terrorist attacks, asteroid hits, et cetera—that may foreclose the possibility of finding a job for the immediate future or at least call for a revision of the daily plan. I refuse, however, to dress up as if heading for a real office, clinging to my usual preclothes, meaning a cross between the T-shirt I wore to bed and the gym clothes I will need in the afternoon.

9:00–12:30: Proceed to desk for the bulk of the day's work—read e-mail, revise résumé, visit the various national job boards, and whatever else I can think of to do. Thanks to the Atlanta Job Search Network I have signed up for, which showers me with several dozen job possibilities a week, e-mail alone can take up to twenty minutes. Why Atlanta? Because it's a happening place, job-wise anyway, with an unemployment rate of only about 4 percent—far lower than Boston, for example, or New York. That and the fact that it's one plane ride away from home qualify it as an appealing target for me. Unfortunately, the job tips that come to me by e-mail from the Atlanta Job Search Network are almost always in irrelevant fields like "systems management" and "construction oversight," but there are sometimes more interesting things to read—brief waves, or cries for help, from my fellow seekers. Trinita, for example, writes sadly (to me and everyone else in the network):

> I have finally found a position, but again it is temporary with no benefits . . . I lost my apartment in Atlanta and had to move home with my mother at the age of 26 after being laid off and unable to pay my bills. I owe everybody and their mama's but I guess I am back on the right track to daylight.

Some of the homespun advice from fellow seekers is equally suggestive of desperation. Mark, whose subject line is "What To DO After You Stop Crying!," lists thirteen activities beginning with "1. Hug your significant other. (Family <u>Must</u> be <u>First</u>!!!)" and ending with:

13. <u>LAST BUT NOT LEAST</u>—Hug your significant other AND KIDS. (<u>REMEMBER</u>—Family MUST be FIRST!!!)

In between, there's the usual enjoinder to network "<u>WITH EVERYONE</u>," including "Aunts, Brothers, Sisters, Cousins, Classmates . . . Accountant, Hair Dresser, Barber, Etc., Etc." and "<u>KEEP A POSITIVE ATTITUDE. DO YOU WANT TO TALK WITH 'DOWN' PEOPLE OR THOSE WHO LIFT YOU UP?</u>"

For weeks, the core of my day's work consists of revising my résumé to meet Joanne's exacting standards. We agree eventually on the opening, which, after every comma has been vetted, reads:

SUMMARY: Seasoned consultant with experience in Event Planning, Public Relations, and Speechwriting is prepared to provide leadership advancing company brand and image. Special expertise in health policy and health-related issues, with a track record of high-level national exposure.

To my chagrin, she informs me that my education is a little scanty. I've listed a BA in chemistry, which I in fact possess, and earned in my maiden name, Alexander. But this is not enough. Surely I have at least audited some relevant courses along the way? So I make up a list of courses I have taken, hoping that they resemble plausible educational offerings, with the idea that I can revise them to suit the situation:

- "Marketing Social Change" (Progressive Media Project, 1991)
- "The Media and New Technology" (New York University, 1995)
- "Writing to Persuade" (New School for Social Research, 1998)
- "Women's Health Issues and the Media" (Long Island University, 1999)
- "The Social Psychology of Event Management" (University of California at Berkeley, 2001)

More vexingly, Joanne wants my résumé to get longer; hers occupies a remarkable four pages. But this is beyond my fictional capacity, so I argue that, no, the résumés posted on the Public Relations Society of America's web site, which I visit daily, are all a terse single page, and that this seems to be the industry standard.

The résumé is still far from perfect, a condition which may take several more weeks of costly coaching to achieve, since both Joanne and Kimberly keep coming up with minor permutations of the latest draft, dithering at length, for example, over what "volunteer community activities" to list. I am beginning to suspect that the process is being artificially prolonged for purely commercial reasons: each half-hour session, which can focus entirely on issues of punctuation and format, earns the coach $100.

Even with an imperfect résumé, as judged by my coaches, I

can't resist applying for some of the jobs that pop up on the PRSA web site. It's easy enough: I just scroll through the PR job offerings—there are usually more than a dozen a week—and send along my résumé-in-progress. I can also apply directly to a company by going to its web site, clicking on "careers," searching for PR job listings, and then submitting my application online. I'll go for anything except the jobs that require technical knowledge—computer networking or video production—or lengthy experience in a particular industry. If all the company seems to want is the ability to think and write, backed by five years of experience, I consider myself a highly qualified candidate, whether the emphasis is on internal communications, publicity, or public affairs. And of course I am admirably flexible, applying at one point for a job as PR director of the American Diabetes Association and then switching sides and offering myself to Hershey's. In most cases, I have the satisfaction of receiving an e-mail automatically confirming my application, and giving me a multidigit number to refer to the job by, should I care to continue the correspondence.

12:30–1:00: Lunch and further newspaper reading, justified by my need, as a PR person, to stay on top of trends, new technologies, business scandals, and the like.

1:00–3:00: Back at the desk for more leisurely or more reflective forms of labor, such as learning more about my chosen fields—PR and event planning—and casting about for further tips and leads. Sometimes the effect of my afternoon labors is to undermine whatever I accomplished in the morning. For example, one day I spend the morning on my résumé and the afternoon reading *Don't Send a Resume: And Other Contrarian Rules to Help Land a Great Job*, by Jeffrey J. Fox, who informs me bleakly:

A resume with a "for everyman" cover letter is junk mail. A resume without a cover letter is used to line the bottom of the birdcage . . . All unexpected and standard resumes go from the IN box to the trash box. Some may generate a rejection form letter; most get ignored; 99.2 percent get tossed.[5]

According to Fox, no one is interested in my background or "career objectives"; all the companies want to know is what I can do for them—which means many more hours at the computer, researching each company in detail, identifying its problems, and dreaming up solutions. Another afternoon's fishing produces the distressing information that employers, especially the large ones, no longer bother to read résumés at all; they scan them with computer programs searching for the desired keywords, and I can only hope that *public relations* and *health* are among them.

3:00–4:30: Proceed to gym for daily workout, as recommended by all coaches and advice-giving web sites. I would work out anyway, but it's nice to have this ratified as a legitimate job-search activity. In fact, I find it expanding to fill the time available—from forty-five minutes to more than an hour a day. I may never find a job, but I will, in a few more weeks, be in a position to wrestle any job competitors to the ground. On the downside, I have no clue as to how to use the gym as a networking opportunity. With whom should I network? The obviously unemployed fellow who circles the indoor track for at least an hour a day? The anorexic gal whose inexplicable utterances on the Stairmaster are not, as I first hoped, attempts

5. Jeffrey J. Fox, *Don't Send a Resume: And Other Contrarian Rules to Help Land a Great Job* (New York: Hyperion, 2001), p. 5.

to communicate but an accompaniment to the songs on her iPod? No matter how many inviting smiles I cast around the place, my conversations never seem to get beyond "Do you mind if I work in?" and "Whoops, I guess that's your towel."

BUT YOU CANNOT spend all your job-search time at the computer. At the Forty-Plus Club, Joe exhorted us, "Get out of your caves!" so I resolve to make an attempt to network with the actually employed. Joanne alerted me to the monthly meetings of a local businesspersons' club just a few miles from home in Charlottesville, at which, for $30, I can get a box lunch and the chance to mingle with current jobholders. I arrive a few minutes late, pockets filled with my business cards, at the hotel meeting room where the session is being held. About seventy people are seated around tables listening to the hotel manager welcome them with a rundown on the hotel's attractions, should anyone decide to check in after lunch and stay for the night: 118 rooms, each with coffeemaker, blow dryer, and ironing board. I guess you could say he is networking too.

A panel of three speakers on the theme "Funding Emerging Growth: Venture Capital and Other Strategies" is introduced, but I am too far back in the room to see them. So, from my vantage point, there are only disembodied male voices to accompany the PowerPoint presentations, all of which highlight the same trend: a dramatic decrease in venture-capital-backed IPOs throughout the state of Virginia since 2001. Everyone seems to handle the bad news with admirable stoicism. There are no interruptions from the audience, no whispers, groans, or attempts to sneak out early. Certain phrases keep recurring—

"skill set," "end of the day," and "due diligence"—which I write down to add to my corporate vocabulary. The only other entertainment possibility is my box lunch, which seems to have been designed as a direct rebuff to the recently deceased Dr. Atkins: chicken salad wrap, macaroni salad, potato chips, and a giant chocolate chip cookie.

Who are these people? Though I'm sitting against the wall in the back of the room, most of the assembled businesspeople are arranged around tables, so quite a few name tags are visible to me and most include company names: CVS, Moneywise Payroll Solutions, WBT Advisors, and a few realty firms. The attached humans are hardly intimidating; I see the same desultory coiffures and dulled, passive expressions you might find at the Forty-Plus Club. It must be that the same corporate culture embraces both jobholders and job seekers, and that it is a culture of conformity and studied restraint, maybe something like that of the Chinese imperial court in the heyday of hardline Confucianism.

But I have to wonder what distinguishes the jobholders as a class. If they don't look any better or radiate any more zest than the job seekers, how come they were chosen for their jobs? Of course, they no doubt possess skills I can barely imagine—in finance, for example, or accounting—and will go back to perform complex, even—from my perspective— occult, activities at their desks.

One person attracts me. A panelist is indulging in a rare attempt at humor, telling us that an SBA (Small Business Administration?) loan cannot be used to fund "strip joints or porno," at which a woman sitting near me mutters "or for overthrowing the government." Funny gal—or hardened revolutionary? I decide she will be my first networking target, but when the program comes to an end she escapes before I can catch her. This leaves me standing near a scary-looking guy of about forty, who is turned out to resemble Michael Douglas in *Wall Street*—well-tailored suit, emerald green silk tie, hair slicked back to a curly fringe brushing against his collar. I should say hi and put out my hand, but he dismisses me with a look of impatience and strides out of the room. I should go up to someone else then, but they are all moving in clumps toward the cloakroom. I smile at anyone whose eye I can catch, but everyone is hastening to reclaim their coats. What do I do? Start thrusting my Kinko's cards into their hands? Throw them up in the air and let people scramble to claim them?

There's nothing to do but get my coat and return to the car as friendless as when I arrived. Maybe Kimberly, if she had been perched on the cheap chandeliers lighting the meeting room, could have told me where I went wrong. But for now I only note with relief that the search part of the day is over and the time has come to repair to the gym.

Lesson learned: I am not ready for the next step, the step that involves face-to-face interactions with people who might actually have jobs to offer. There's the matter of my business cards, for example. It's the end of January, and in two months I have managed to give away no more than five out of 100 of them. I understand that with respect to the cards, my job is like that of those guys on the streets of Manhattan who try to hit you with deli menus—the point is simply to get rid of them. Until the cards are out there, fluttering around in the world, I might as well not exist. But to hand out even a single card, I would have to engage someone in conversation long enough for it to seem natural to say, "Here, why don't you take one of my cards?" Something is holding me back—maybe "lack of confidence," as Kimberly and I agree to call it, though I suspect also a prideful resistance to "selling myself."

Other job seekers seem to suffer from the same reticence. Hillary Meister, for example, whom I met by e-mail through the Atlanta Job Search Network, says she has trouble with "the whole networking thing":

> It's personality. I'm very quiet, not very extroverted. It [networking] feels so fake to me, but I know that's the game.

It feels "fake" because we know it involves the deflection of our natural human sociability to an ulterior end. Normally we meet strangers in the expectation that they may truly be strange, and are drawn to the multilayered mystery that each human presents. But in networking, as in prostitution, there is no time for fascination. The networker is always, so to speak, looking over the shoulder of the person she engages in conversation, toward whatever concrete advantage can be gleaned from the interaction—a tip or a precious contact. This instrumentalism undermines the possibility of a group identity, say, as white-collar victims of corporate upheaval. No matter how crowded the room, the networker prowls alone, scavenging to meet his or her individual needs.

These objections, though, are in the present circumstances only excuses. Whatever is holding me back—shyness or pride—it must be vanquished, and in this enterprise I can see I need further help.

The Forty-Plus Club's boot camp is not an option. On my next trip to D.C. for its Monday-morning get-together, Ted confronts me with the question "What's holding you back?" I freeze, sure that this is a Joe-type query to which the possible responses include "procrastination" and "nonlinear career path." "Money?" he continues, and I realize he's asking what holds me back from enlisting in the boot camp. I say no, I can't commute two and a half hours each way every weekday for three weeks of 9–5 sessions.

"There's a guy who commuted all the way from Pennsylvania," Ted reproaches me. "Or you could stay in a hotel."

If I went through boot camp, I would be entitled to become an actual member of the club, which might put me in a position to hang out with Merle, exchange views on the correct hanging of scarves over suit jackets, and absorb some of her executive aura for myself. But I have found an appealingly condensed alternative; or rather it has found me. One day when I was weeding through the Atlanta job possibilities, I came across an announcement for an "executive boot camp" to be hosted by something called the ExecuTable and scheduled to take exactly one day. It isn't cheap, especially when you factor in airfare and a night in a hotel, but the difference between 7 hours and the 120-hour commitment required by Forty-Plus is compelling. So I go to Travelocity.com and, after about thirty minutes of comparative shopping, come up with a travel plan.

three

Surviving Boot Camp

I've been to Atlanta twice in the last two years, just long enough to gain the impression that it's a city without a heart. From one of the downtown hotels I stayed in on a previous trip, I could walk two blocks in any direction without encountering another pedestrian. I even asked the doorman where the Atlantans could be found, and he directed me to take the subway out to a mall in the suburbs, where indeed there were hundreds of people, none of them showing signs of having recently fled a neutron bomb attack. This could be the latest urban trend—the depopulated effect—since I've encountered it also in Dallas and Oklahoma City. What it means, for the unemployed, is that there are no public spaces in which to congregate, have a coffee, and maybe strike up a conversation. The only options are home, workplace, or mall; and if you have no source of income, the mall is not recommended. But the boot camp is to be held in the thriving northeastern suburbs, where life apparently goes on.

I arrive in Atlanta with something less than a winning attitude. It's already February, and I have precious little to show for my time. I've been laboring steadily away on my résumé with Joanne, which has become a project on the scale of a graduate thesis, and—after endless tweakings and arguments over how best to highlight my strong points—she has pronounced me "almost there," maybe just because I've let her know I'm not willing to pay for another month of her services. I have furthermore posted this nearly finished product on Monster and HotJobs.com and sent it off to a dozen major pharmaceutical companies—from Abbot to Wyeth—that are looking for PR people and allow you to apply right on the company web sites. Confident, at this point, that my résumé includes all the requisite skills, I expand beyond the pharmas and leap to offer myself to any company seeking:

> [an] experienced and highly motivated Director of Communications. Duties include branding organization throughout local corporate community, creating general community awareness, media outreach and creation of promotional materials.

Or perhaps:

> [a] skilled writer with solid professional editing and communications strategy skills (health care communicatins exp. is a big plus). You will have at least 2 yrs of exp. (w/sample portofilio) that includes working w/media. Must possess a BA degree.

A couple of companies send me automatic acknowledgments by e-mail, and one—Wyeth—goes so far as to send me an actual postcard. That's it, though; for the most part, corporate America seems willing to soldier on without my help.

In my declining frame of mind, even boot camp has begun to loom as a test I may very likely fail. Do I have the mental stamina for the boot-camp experience? What if it's conducted in incomprehensible corporate jargon? Is there a chance that, in the intensity of the day's interactions, I'll be exposed as a fraud?

We sit, about fifteen of us, around a horseshoe-shaped table facing our leader, Patrick Knowles. Based on the number of times the word *executive* came up in the web description of the boot camp and in one brief phone conversation with Patrick, during which he requested a résumé as a condition for attendance, I pictured something a bit more imposing than a windowless meeting room in the ultraminimalist Hampton Inn. There aren't even any water glasses at our places or free pads to write on. I am hoping we will go around the table and introduce ourselves, though there are only a few exceptions to the usual blank corporate look. I cannot help but wonder about James (identified by the name card in front of him), for example, if only because of his crazy overgrown crew cut, or Billy, a handsome man in his forties who seems a little too tightly wound for the occasion, almost straining to contain his excitement. And there's the enigmatic Cynthia, a tousled redhead of about forty-five, who manages to look fastidious and slightly remote even in blue jeans. But there are no introductions, and we leap right in.

Patrick, who had boomed confidently on the phone, is not

the commanding presence I pictured. Partly bald, with color-
less, protuberant eyes and a distinctly uncorporate paunch, he
begins on an oddly therapeutic note:

> I'm going to make eye contact with you. You need to trust and
> see where this experience will take you. It's based on experi-
> ential learning, which has three parts: visual, auditory, and
> kinesthetic. There are four major questions: What do you
> want your life to look like a year from now? What challenges
> do you face to make that happen? What commitments do you
> need to make to face those challenges? What is the price
> you're going to pay if you don't make those commitments?

Three parts and four questions—except for the eye contact
part, it all sounds dismayingly Morton-like. The difference is
that, despite his appearance, Patrick has charisma; the more he
talks, the more energy he absorbs, apparently from the vibra-
tions of his own voice in the room, since there is not the slightest stirring of response from the group.

> I want to tell you my philosophy. It's very powerful. *Every unit
> increase in your personal sense of well-being increases your ex-
> ternal performance exponentially.*

This proposition is expressed on the flip chart as
"*EP/PSWB*." We're only five minutes into the day's work, and
already I'm straining to understand. If *EP*, meaning external
performance, varies exponentially with *PSWB*—one's personal
sense of well-being—why are we interested in the *ratio* of *EP*
to *PSWB*? Over the course of the day, this central proposition
will take various pseudomathematical forms, such as "*EP*

10+/*PSWB*" and "*EP* 10ˣ/*PSWB*," driving me nuts. Of course I am losing sight of the fact that neither *EP* nor *PSWB* can be expressed in numerical form; at least I can't imagine how you would quantify your personal sense of well-being. But, although the room turns out to contain several IT and telecom guys who must have some glancing acquaintance with mathematics, or at least with logical, digital-type thinking, no one else seems remotely bothered. The point is to pump that *PSWB* up.

> *PSWB* depends on authenticity and congruency and these are reinforced by a journey of self-discovery. You're going to watch people make changes in their lives . . . You have to trust that whatever I do will lead to this [self-discovery.] This is the Knowles group model of experiential coaching.

So this is how the "Knowles group model" operates: We will go around the table, though not in any predictable order, with each person in turn going to the front of the room and addressing the "four questions," under Patrick's vigilant leadership. He tells us that he "has permission" to interrupt us at any moment and say "freeze," upon which we are not to speak or make eye contact with others. Who gave him "permission"? Certainly not the people in the room, most of whom seem to have already been frozen into a state of dull acquiescence. As at the Forty-Plus Club, the prevailing emotional tone is depression, leavened with timid expectation. Anyway, this "freezing" business is called "pattern interruption," and, Patrick tells us, "it's very powerful." The purpose is to "get value from experience," as if experience were a novel new place to find "value."

First up is Richard, who is about sixty and has a kindly face etched with permanent wince lines. He had been in real estate but left that field for undisclosed reasons, seemingly having to do with its being "so high pressure." Then he realized his life-long dream of going into business with his son, but "that didn't work out." This is a trend, I've read: unemployed parents going to work in their grown children's businesses. It can be a risky undertaking, involving, as it does, the overthrow of long-standing parental authority; and I can think of nothing sadder than to be fired by one's own child on the threshold of old age. What Richard's looking for now is fairly cosmic: "some direction for my life."

All this is delivered in a flat tone, without the slightest self-pity but with an expression suggesting that Richard is accustomed to having his utterances answered with slaps. I am afraid he'll start to cry or at least put his hands up over his face to ward off oncoming blows, but, mercifully, Patrick "freezes" him before any more failures can be confessed, telling us, "I have to dig the pain out, but he's very tender; I can't push too hard." We are all asked to comment on Richard's condition, and the overeager Billy, who turns out to have spent most of his life in the military, observes briskly, "They want ten to fourteen hours a day now," apparently referring to the high-pressure real estate job. "It's a challenge."

"They?" Patrick interrupts. "Who are *they?*"

It turns out that we are not to talk about "them"; we are to confine ourselves to speaking "experientially." But Cynthia, the redhead, who turns out to be a real estate agent, makes the same mistake, commenting that "Richard's taking personally the fact that the real estate market is so awful." Patrick ignores this sensible interjection. The market is of no interest to us; it's just another "they"—some external force or entity that can be used as an excuse for our failures.

This lesson is reinforced with Kevin, who says he is thirty-six and a practitioner of something called "operations management." Poor Kevin—who offers, as his most positive self-endorsement, that he is "dependable"—now faces rumors of impending layoffs at his firm and is contemplating a leap into his own business. But this won't be easy, because he has two children and a nonworking wife. Suddenly, as if losing patience, Patrick "freezes" Kevin and turns to us: "The person who is stopping Kevin is who?"

Everyone, myself excepted, answers in unison: "Kevin!"

Somehow Kevin's plight inspires Patrick to launch into an anecdote about his college friend Mitch. Years ago, when they were both young, they had gone to Mitch's house for Thanksgiving dinner. Patrick sets the scene carefully: Outside it was cold and slushy. Inside, the house was warm, filled with enticing cooking smells. Before dinner, he and Mitch decided to sneak into the kitchen and make turkey sandwiches for themselves. They were gleefully stuffing themselves when Patrick heard a crash behind him. Mitch had fallen to the floor. Patrick thought that this must have been another one of Mitch's pranks, but Mitch was lying there turning blue. He had had a stroke. As a result he became disfigured and unable to speak for months. But guess what? *He* is Mitch. Mitch is really Patrick.

And this shows . . . Well, he went through this terrible struggle in rehab to learn to speak again. Patrick pauses, lost in some personal zone. What it shows is, well—and all he can come up with is "the importance of being understood."

Baffled by the anecdote, we are dismissed into the hotel

lobby for a break over coffee and juice supplied by the Hampton. I introduce myself to James, the wild-haired guy, explaining that I've only been searching for a couple of months.

"Welcome to the land of the undead," he says, adding that he's been looking for a telecommunications job for over a year.

I ask what he made of the story, and he shrugs, wondering only why Patrick had changed his name from Mitch. My theory, which I do not share, is that somewhere along the line Patrick heard a similar narrative from a motivational speaker: there was this boy who grew up in poverty and was abused all the time and had a learning disability to boot, and guess what? That boy was me.

Patrick must have liked the device enough to apply it, however sloppily, to himself. But the details need some tweaking. What were they doing carving up the turkey for sandwiches just before dinner? No matter how hungry you are, the carving of the turkey is a ritual activity, performed at the table on an intact bird. And why was the kitchen empty at this crucial moment when the potato mashing and gravy making should be in full swing? I would like to share these questions, but they might seem unkind. James, anyway, has exhausted his interest in the topic and moved on to the juice dispenser, while Cynthia is sharing with me her concern about confidentiality. I agree, it's hard to let down your guard if you don't know the people, and at this point I see no reason to trust Patrick himself. Boot camp seems to be structured like group therapy, but the most challenging case in the group may be that of our leader.

Back from our break, we hear from a thirtysomething woman who "loves" her job as a hospital administrator but can no longer keep up with the hours, given the demands of motherhood, and would rather do something more meaningful and "people oriented" anyway. Patrick has nothing to suggest except that she should keep a journal of "major events, thoughts, and feelings of the day," and moves on to a large, deflated-looking fellow who speaks poignantly of having been the "go-to guy" in his branch of the trade show industry until he lost his business in the wake of 9/11 and turned into "nothing." Then there's Chris, a sad-faced telecommunications guy in his late thirties, who is tired of the excessive demands of his job and hearing the drumbeats of layoffs all around him.

I am surprised at how many of my fellow campers are actually employed, at least at the moment, since I had expected to be surrounded by jobless seekers like myself. But the white-collar workforce seems to consist of two groups: those who can't find work at all and those who are employed in jobs where they work much more than they want to. In between lies a scary place where you dedicate long hours to a job that you sense is about to eject you, if only because so many colleagues have been laid off already. I've read about a form of depression called "survivor syndrome," which is said to be rampant in layoff-prone firms, and several of these campers would seem to be among the victims. In Chris's case, no solutions are offered, though he is instructed to "own his experience."

Now it's my turn. I had hoped to go a little later in the day, when I would have had more time to study the other campers' performances and mentally rehearse my own, but here I am, plucked straight out of my reverie and marched to the front of the room. I keep my self-description brief: that I've been an event planner and public relations person on a consulting basis and am now seeking the security, continuity, and camaraderie of a corporate job, though, listening to them, I wonder if I'm not heading in the wrong direction, since a lot of them seem as eager to escape the corporate world as I am to enter it.

This fails to elicit even a nod of acknowledgment from my audience, so I move on swiftly to my "challenges," listing, first, my age, and, second, my fear that I won't fit into the corporate culture, because I'm beginning to sense that there is one, and that I may be just too flippant, sarcastic, and impatient for it. I feel, I say, like I'm supposed to force myself into a mold. At this, Patrick interrupts to "freeze" me, an assault that I, automatically and without the slightest forethought, ham up—raising my hands and jerking backward as if immobilized by a laser gun. *What's wrong with Barbara?* is the question on the floor, although Patrick doesn't put it quite so baldly.

First he blows off the age issue. He himself is fifty-nine (although it should be noted here that, when I see him a month later, he will be fifty-eight). As for the personality issue, Patrick appears incensed that I would suggest that there is a corporate culture we have to conform to. "You can't remake yourself. You have to find the one place out there that will nurture and value YOU!"

Breaking out of my frozen condition, I object that there are hundreds of thousands of companies out there, so how do I find my "one place"? His response is to recommend that I create a "support group" to function as my "team." I am now officially unfrozen and sent back to my seat to write all this wisdom down. Billy speaks up to advise me that *T-E-A-M* means "Together Everyone Achieves More," and that *F-E-A-R* means "False Evidence . . ." but I miss the rest of it. Patrick wraps up my case with the Zen-like pronouncement: "The point is, it's whatever you make of it."

I am both relieved to be out of the spotlight and dismayed at the uselessness of Patrick's advice. For this I paid $179 and flew all the way to Atlanta? But we are on to James, who, it turns out, is the one real rebel in the room. He describes himself, calmly and confidently, as a "thinker, communicator, writer, instructor." In short, he's a "philosopher." "Plato, Socrates, and Nietzsche are dead, but I'm here."

There is a shocked silence in the room until, after a few beats, Patrick recovers himself enough to ask what James's "challenge" is.

"To market myself," he says, and I struggle to imagine these words coming out of Socrates' mouth.

"You need to add clarity to your message," Patrick counsels.

The others are far harsher: "Where's the bottom line?" someone asks. "Where's the value added?" Billy throws in, and someone adds the sniffy judgment "Not too practical!"

I can't resist jumping in to defend James: Look, I say, you're trying to squeeze him into the corporate mold! You're not letting James be what he is! I would like to say I did this solely out of the desire to defend philosophy over telecommunications, but mostly I'm just vindicating myself: there *is* a mold! James, although now officially "frozen," picks up on my support, insisting he will not remake himself to fit into the corporate world. For the first time so far, the group laughs. "You like to eat?" "You win the lottery?"

But James's response to my intervention on his behalf sets off a train of thought that entertains me through Patrick's ramblings all the way to lunch. If I could win James over, could I organize the whole group to rebel against Patrick and *his* philosophy? Cynthia could probably be won over, and possibly Chris, who confided to me during the break that he's "tired of making other people rich," possibly Patrick included. Billy, however, would be a problem, since he seems to be somehow in league with Patrick or at least a little too invested in the program.

Among the other irritating features of the boot camp, I'm getting tired of Patrick's self-advertisements, as when he confides that he has "the same skill set as Dr. Phil," the TV guru, and lacks only a backer like Oprah. The boot camp, I'm beginning to see, serves up recruits for his personal coaching sessions, just as the sessions have generated at least four of the campers. Those who have already been through his personal coaching, like Ken, a pleasant-looking forty-something who remains silent throughout the day, are praised lavishly for their "progress" compared to some earlier condition, and the rest of us are not too subtly encouraged to undergo the individual coaching ourselves. It's unclear why the graduates of Patrick's personal coaching are here at all, unless just to pad out the session for the rest of us, making Patrick seem to be more in demand than he is. As for his philosophy, it's straightforward victim blaming: your problem is *you,* which is of course the only thing Patrick, with his ad hoc blend of pop-psych insights, is prepared to take on anyway.

At the lunch break I find myself a fairly popular girl; Cynthia wants to eat with me, so do Billy and James; Kevin and Richard tag along. After a scuffle, my choice of a nearby diner prevails over Chik-Fil-A, giving us about forty minutes to chat over burgers and salady substances. James reveals that he's just refinanced his house. Billy explains that he's transitioning from aviation to career coaching and will soon be starting up a networking group of his own. When I mention my possible relocation to Atlanta, he looks at me forcefully and says, "Tea," in a tone that suggests I should surrender my glass of the iced beverage to him at once. But no, this is another acronym—Thought, Emotion, Action—which he explains is a military notion. Meanwhile, Kevin is busy making logistical-sounding calls on his cell phone. "Working on Saturday?" "No," he tells me, "Cub Scouts."

In the car on the way back to the Hampton, I tell James that I was surprised he brought up Nietzsche, who seemed, well, a little out of place here. "Patrick's philosophy is so upbeat and positive, but Nietzsche's outlook was"—I struggle to come up with a word that might locate the author of *Thus Spake Zarathustra* in the same conceptual universe as Patrick Knowles—"you know, kind of tragic."

"Well, he was really smart anyway" is James's rejoinder.

I can only agree, and urge James to continue on his chosen path, no matter what the philistines say.

After lunch, it's Cynthia's turn. She describes herself as "living on the edge . . . seeing life as an adventure," but there's more defensiveness than bravado in this, as if she's anticipating a rebuke. The problem is she's burned out on real estate; the market has collapsed, and she can't break even. She's putting longer and longer hours into the company but finding herself losing ground financially every month. "What should I do with my life?" is the question that brought her here. "What do I want to do when I grow up?" She has some dim notion of the direction she would like to take: "I'm a people person—passionately—and I want to help people."

All this sounds pretty unexceptional to me—an unrewarding job, a desire for more socially useful employment—but Patrick leaps in with a psychiatric diagnosis: Cynthia is suffering from "low-grade depression" and "feelings of loss that aren't career related at all." To my alarm, she starts to cry, confessing with tears rolling down her cheeks that her father just died and that a long-term relationship broke off only a few months ago.

In a softened tone, Patrick admits that he knew about these life crises from a prior one-on-one session with Cynthia but professes to have "forgotten" them and based his diagnosis entirely on her current demeanor. He sits down directly across from her with one hand on her knee and the other lower down on her crossed leg, which looks to me like borderline harassment. The cure for Cynthia is further one-on-one coaching with him, which he urges her to undertake immediately. As for the rest of us, he advises: "Extrapolate to your own experiences. She's you; you're her." All, in other words, in need of further coaching.

So he set her up. Maybe she had cried during her private session with him, where he had learned what buttons to press, because there's nothing like tears to give group therapy a veneer of intensity and hard-won "growth." If I am indeed her, then I am entitled to the resentment this little drama has inspired in me. I blame myself too, though, because she must have wanted to have lunch with me alone, and by letting all the guys troop along, I may have brushed off a bid for sisterly support.

After Cynthia, the afternoon sours for me. The air has grown stuffy with postprandial exhalations and deodorant breakthroughs. My back hurts from sitting so long—whatever happened to the "kinesthetic" part of this experience? One after another, the remaining campers are processed and dismissed. Allan, who was downsized after twenty years at an investment firm, is told, "It's not about getting a job"—an observation so important that Patrick repeats it. "It's *not* about getting a job. It's about knowing yourself . . . The issue is Allan knowing who Allan is."

Jason, who feels he has very little to show for his forty-two years and is now facing the near-certainty of a layoff, is scolded, as I was, for even mentioning the age issue: "It's all internal—whether you're sixty-two or forty-two or twenty-two . . . It's never about the external world. It's always between you and you." Thus we are sealed into our own version of Plato's cave—wrestling blindly with what Patrick construes as our failings, deprived of even the slightest glimpse of the waning afternoon light outside.

At the afternoon break, Cynthia rushes off, with only a rueful glance in exchange for my belated commiserations. In the lobby where we stand around a coffee machine, there's a TV tuned to CNN's coverage of some celebrity CEO's trial, and I laughingly suggest to Billy that there ought to be plenty of demand for PR people, given all the corporate scandals.

"I blame it all on the last administration," he says gravely.

"On Clinton?"

"Yes, his behavior."

"With Monica?" I'm confused. "How is that on a scale of these multimillion-dollar thefts?"

"Clinton was responsible for twenty-seven deaths."

"Huh?" I quickly search my internal database of right-wing conspiracy theories. "You mean like Vince Foster?"

"And other people he knew. Check it out."

"And Bush isn't responsible for any deaths?"

"That's war."

I start in on the war before biting my tongue in midsentence. Why I am arguing with him? I have no hard-and-fast rules to govern my behavior here, other than to keep a low profile and get as much job-related information as possible. But political discussions are clearly beyond the pale, even if I am itching for a fight.

In his wrap-up, Patrick writes the word *MAGIC* on the board, with the letters running downward. This too is an acronym: Making decisions, greater Accountability, Growth, reduce your Isolation, deal with issues of Change. He puts yet another version of the *EP/PSWB* formula on the board, repeating that *PSWB* is based on "authenticity" and "congruency." I finally venture to ask what congruency means in this context, and am told that it "means to do it in a consistent fashion." OK, whatever. The man who lost his trade show business after 9/11 turns up his hands in a gesture of acceptance and offers his own summary: "We have met the enemy, and he is us."

We break up with vague promises to stay in touch; Patrick himself will be calling each of us in the coming week "as a means of accountability," though to whom remains undefined. I step out of the Hampton lobby to discover that the sky has cleared and that the sun is already low behind the Holiday Inn, a couple of blocks away, where my suitcase is stashed. A wind has come up, a little too cold for my fashionably thin new winter coat, but welcome nonetheless. Yes, Patrick, of course, we make our own lives, but we make them out of *something*. The wind bites my face; the pavement pushes back against my feet. There is an external world after all, and if you can't feel yourself pressing up against the resistance, how do you know that you're moving at all?

ONE OF MY subsidiary missions, in the weeks that follow, is to try to get a better grip on Patrick's strangely ghostly world-view. If the belief is widespread, in the corporate culture, that there's no external world of any consequence, that we are responsible for everything that happens to us, then I should know this and perhaps be prepared to expound it myself. There's certainly a heavy dose of Mary Baker Eddy in it, and the mind-over-matter philosophy embodied in her Christian Science. Nor should we omit Norman Vincent Peale and his mid-twentieth-century opus *The Power of Positive Thinking.* Mostly, though, what Patrick's weltanschauung puts me in mind of is EST, the pop-psych fad that bubbled out of the hot tubs of Esalen in the seventies and into the executive suites, with the message that you and you alone are responsible for your fate. It's a long-standing American idea, in other words, that circumstances count for nothing compared to the power of the individual will.

I order one of the books Patrick recommended to us, which is seductively titled *The Ultimate Secret to Getting Absolutely Everything You Want,* although focused almost entirely on the getting of money. When he wrote the first edition of the book in the early eighties, the author, Mike Hernacki, tells us, $1 million was an appropriate goal. Now, however, "you really can't call yourself rich . . . unless you have at least three million bucks." So that's where the bar is set; now how to get over it? We have to start by acknowledging something that "may be difficult, even painful to look at":

> You must recognize that *you alone* are the source of all the conditions and situations in your life. You must recognize that whatever your world looks like right now, *you alone* have caused it to look that way. The state of your health, your

finances, your personal relationships, your professional life—all of it is *your* doing, yours and no one else's.[1]

Lest this sentiment sound like a psychotic delusion, the blurbs on the cover of the book announce that it is shared, or at least has been endorsed, by Norman Vincent Peale and Mark Victor Hansen, coauthor of the *Chicken Soup for the Soul* series. More troublingly, from a personal standpoint, there is also a blurb from a senior vice president of PaineWebber (now UBS), the company that handles my Keogh plan. I can only hope that its employees retain some dim sense that the market is not entirely an emanation of their interior lives.

Reading along, I discover how it is that our thoughts and desires mold the world around us. "Things attract other things," meaning that there is a kind of gravitational force connecting our thoughts to their real-world fulfillments. "Whenever you think something, the thought immediately attracts its physical equivalent." Thus, for example, the thought of $3 million can be relied on to exert a powerful attractive force on whatever currency may be lying around, and this force actually increases in strength as the dollar bills get closer. How can this be? By way of explanation, Hernacki enlists some physics in the form of the law of gravitational attraction:

$$F = GM_1M_2/R^2$$

Here, the *M*'s are the masses of the two attracting objects; *G* is the gravitational constant, and *R* is the distance between them.

1. Mike Hernacki, *The Ultimate Secret to Getting Absolutely Everything You Want* (New York: Berkley, 2001), pp. xii, 47.

Obviously, as *R*—say, the distance between you and the money—gets smaller, *F,* the force attracting the money, gets radically larger. Confused? Hernacki is reassuring.

> Now, I congratulate you if you were able to follow that discussion and understand the mathematics of this phenomenon. But if you didn't understand a word of it, don't worry. All you have to do is think the thought. Simply by saying the word, you put the law of attraction into motion. The rest is taken care of, automatically and with accelerating acceleration.[2]

Appallingly, he has even screwed up the purloined physics here: the *acceleration* is not accelerating; only the *motion* accelerates. But what am I nitpicking for? No dollars are flying into my pockets at any detectable speed.

I move on from Hernacki's physics of wish fulfillment to *Before You Think Another Thought* by Bruce I. Doyle III, which, Amazon.com informs me, is popular with Hernacki's readers. In this slender book, we no longer find gravity connecting thoughts to their real-life equivalents, which is somewhat reassuring, since thoughts of course have no mass (meaning that Hernacki's *F* is always and inevitably zero).[3] In

---

2. Hernacki, *The Ultimate Secret*, pp. 90, 95.
3. In yet another scheme, which was forwarded to members of the Atlanta Job Search Network, it is magnetism that connects our desires to their fulfillment: "Dr. Karl Pribram, the respected neuropsychologist, has found that . . . the 'law of attraction' is alive and well and working within the mind of every human being. Dr. Pribram discovered that any visual image, imagined in complete detail, sets up a force field of energy that begins to attract into your life the people, ideas, things and even circumstances that are consistent with that image. If you visualize a positive outcome . . . you begin to exert a powerful magnetic force that brings the desired goal or outcome into reality."

Doyle's scheme, thoughts fulfill themselves without help from any intervening force, and they can do this because each "thoughtform" is really "a minute wave of energy . . . operat[ing] faster than the speed of light." Fortunately for us, "the mission of each thoughtform is to fulfill the intent of the thought," and it does so "by attracting similar thoughtforms to help it fulfill itself." How do you make your dreams come true? Simply by beaming them out from your mind. "Scientifically," Doyle asserts—and it is hard to think of a setting in which that adverb has been more flagrantly abused—"one might say that focusing your attention on the energy field of consciousness, which contains the waves of all possibilities, creates the particles (events and materializations) that you experience as your reality."[4]

Among other things, these books explain the importance of the "winning attitude" I have been urged to adopt: a positive attitude "attracts" or "fulfills," depending on which author's weird science you go with, positive results, with little or no action on your part required. Herein, too, lies the answer to the question I once posed to Kimberly: would it be enough to just fake a winning attitude? No way, according to Doyle:

> People who just pretend to have a positive attitude may be more acceptable, but they will still attract according to how they are really vibrating—the energy they are emanating will attract their circumstances.[5]

4. Bruce I. Doyle III, *Before You Think Another Thought* (Winter Park, FL: Rare Shares Ltd., 1994), pp. 18, 19, 48.
5. Ibid., p. 67.

The obvious liberal rejoinders come to mind: What about the child whose home is hit by a bomb? Did she have some bomb-shaped thoughtform that brought ruin down on her head? And did my boot-camp mates cause the layoffs that drove them out of their jobs by "vibrating" at a layoff-related frequency? It seems inexcusably cruel to tell people who have reached some kind of personal nadir that their problem is entirely of their own making. I find my thoughtforms massing for an attack on Hernacki, Doyle, and Knowles—pummeling them, knocking them to the ground, all the while accusing them of unconsciously bringing this assault on themselves. Because how else could anything happen to these fellows, except through their own will and desire?

But from the point of view of the economic "winners"—those who occupy powerful and high-paying jobs—the view that one's fate depends entirely on oneself must be remarkably convenient. It explains the winners' success in the most flattering terms while invalidating the complaints of the losers. Patrick's clients, for example, came to the boot camp prepared to blame their predicament on the economy, or the real estate market, or the inhuman corporate demands on their time. But these culprits were summarily dismissed in favor of alleged individual failings: depression, hesitation, lack of focus. It's not the world that needs changing, is the message, it's *you*. No need, then, to band together to work for a saner economy or a more human-friendly corporate environment, or to band together at all. As one of my fellow campers put it, we are our own enemies.

But it's all too easy for me to sneer at the EST-minded gurus. When I get past my revulsion, the boot-camp experience and subsequent reading have one clear lesson for me in my role as a job seeker, and that is that I may not be *doing enough*. If I don't find a job, and that is the goal I set for myself, it may in fact be my own fault. I resolve to try harder, do more, put those thoughtforms to work! I need to get out more, network more, and network with people who have more to offer me than the unhappy crew assembled by Knowles.

SEARCHING FOR NETWORKING opportunities closer to home— and hopefully closer to the people who do the actual hiring—I come across a conveniently timed ExecuNet meeting in Richmond, designed to help retool executives "in transition." When I call to inquire, I am asked about my salary expectations, and this time, in a surge of positive thinking, I say $100,000. But that turns out to be half as much as what you need to get into the Richmond confab; for pikers like me, there's another meeting in Washington. The cost is a mere $35, plus the $150 I've already spent to become an ExecuNet member and receive its monthly newsletter—a small price to pay, I guess, to network with a superior class of people. I am advised to bring forty copies of my résumé and to dress in business clothes. But when I get to Washington, the latter instruction is overruled by the weather: given that it's freezing cold with icy patches on the sidewalks and a five-block walk between the Metro station and my hotel, I go in slacks and sneakers, though the upper body is, I think, respectably put together.

Ah, sweet luxury! The get-together takes place in an upper-middle-type hotel, at least $100 a night beyond the Hampton Inn, in a spacious conference room where an entire buffet awaits us: fruit and cheese, egg rolls, satay sticks, coffee, and soda. All we are missing, one of my fellow job seekers observes, is the wine. Before the program begins, we have half an hour to network, which is easy enough to do since there are only five—not the promised forty—other people present, and there's no way for anyone to escape my overtures. Paul, a deadly pale, thirtyish fellow, tells me that he is still reeling from a conversation he had with his boss last week, who warned him of a coming wave of layoffs and that he, Paul, was likely to be let go, if only because he is paid more than anyone else in the department. His title is impressive—director of business development—and he must earn over $100,000 to be here. But success, in his case, has had a perverse effect.

I also approach Donald, who unnerves me by starting with, "I know I've seen you somewhere before!" Before he can recall that the previous sighting must have been on TV, someone intervenes to tease Donald about his "dumb pickup line." A laid-off sales and marketing VP with a wife and three children to support, Donald confides that he's been through "some very wild emotional mood swings. I've gotten defocused, kind of hiding from my reality." But he seems to have absorbed the EST-like ideology of the job seekers' world, reporting, "Now I'm totally past any sort of victim mentality, which is so dysfunctional."

When we are seated comfortably around the table, Ron, our leader for the evening, introduces himself. He identifies himself as a "serial entrepreneur" who has launched all sorts of small companies providing business services. The high point of his career seems to have been the years he spent at the RNC (Republican National Committee), though he assures us, "I don't go around with a big *R* on my chest," perhaps on the off chance that there might be a Democrat present. I don't hold that against him, but if I had to "design," as Kimberly might put it, an RNC operative, Ron would be it. He has the burnished skin of a man who can afford regular facials, and a collar so tight that his face puffs out alarmingly from the neck. As he speaks, his eyes slither warily from one of us to another, reminding me of the Time Warner executives I once lunched with years ago, who seemed poised at all times between arrogance and deference, nervously calculating which to project. A line from a Robert Lowell poem comes to mind: "a savage servility/slides by on grease."

"There are four ways to find a job," Ron is explaining: "networking, networking, networking, and networking." As for posting your résumé on job boards like Monster.com—don't bother, if only because you'll want to send a customized résumé for each job you apply for. I can only wonder what "customizing" involves and how much it borders on fraud. Tim, the sandy-haired man on my right, who has carried Ron's tight-collar theme to what looks like a painful extreme, chimes in to testify that in thirty years as a VP of HR, he never posted a job advertisement on a board. Donald observes that the boards are for "your fifty-K people and below." Apparently, in the exalted circle I have entered here, all jobs are attained through personal contacts.

Continuing his introduction, Ron reveals that he does not actually work for ExecuNet, but for some other firm called McCarthy and Company, which is in possession of 300 high-level networking contacts. The purpose of this evening's program is to teach us how to make use of such contacts, should we be inspired to pay McCarthy for the right to pursue them.

But any sense of having arrived at some place of comfortable superiority evaporates with a comment from Neal, a fortyish former media manager with an Australian accent and unruly blond hair. Sounding like a thousand blues songs, he says, "I wake up and say, 'Oh God, another morning' . . . I have no focus." *Focus,* I am beginning to realize, is a code word for an emotional rather than a cognitive state; to lose it is to be not just confused or distracted but seriously depressed. Patrick would have come to life at Neal's admission of despair—digging into him to find the buried depression, challenging him to confront, of course, Neal.

Ron, however, is impervious to desperation; the secret of focus, he says, is "to make the search process like going into the office, whether that means going to the library, to a friend's house, or to our [McCarthy's] office." Furthermore, you have to have someone to "keep you accountable," meaning a surrogate boss-figure. "We're used to having bosses, being responsive to someone, so you've got to create the same dynamic."

Neal appears unmollified by this advice, which of course I recognize from the Forty-Plus meeting: turn your job search into a job, and not just a freelance-type job. You have to structure it hierarchically, complete with someone playing the role of boss, preferably a paid coach like Ron. Thus the one great advantage of unemployment—the freedom to do as you please, to get up when you want, wear what you want, and let your mind drift here and there—is foreclosed. Just when you finally have a chance to be fully autonomous and possibly creative, for a few months anyway, you have to invent a little drama in which you are still toiling away for the man. The arrangement brings to mind Erich Fromm's best-seller of the fifties, *Escape from Freedom,* which was an attempt to understand the appeal of fascism. What clearer sign of an aversion to freedom than actually paying someone to play the role of your boss?

Ron opens the session up for questions, and Donald asks whether he should mention a recent illness, which cost him three months of work, to prospective employers. Ron's advice: "Turn [the illness] into a sound bite that could be positive for you." Emboldened by Donald, I ask, "What if you've lost time due to homemaking and raising children?" Ron replies:

> The challenge is to be a beggar with a great story. If that story doesn't land you [get you a job], you've probably got a values mismatch. Turn it into a compelling story.

A beggar? Well, perhaps that does sum up the status of motherhood in our society. I glance at the one other woman at the table, whose résumé describes her as having spent much of the last decade bringing the idea of "competition" to Latin America for some New York–based bank, but her eyes dart back anxiously to Ron. I must be the only one here who didn't understand that homemaking is such an unusual experience as to require an entertaining explanation. How would I begin my "compelling story"? I met this guy, see, and, uh . . .

Ron goes on to the meat of the evening, though given his metaphors, the main course sounds more like dessert. Recruiters, he counsels, are like the job boards on the Internet—something to be avoided. Ron's "significant other" is a recruiter, and he knows "they won't do much for you unless you can do something for them"—which sends me off into irrelevant fantasies on the subject of Ron's love life. Things are looking up in the job market, he continues, but this will at first cause more competition, as people seek to leave the less-than-desirable "interim jobs" they have found, which is "another reason you've got to be the banana split." All this is delivered in a low-key, noninvasive tone unlike that of any of my previous coaches—just a casual sharing of information among equals. Here's an idea: Write to executives who are profiled in business publications and tell them what their company needs at this stage, which is, of course, you. Tell them how you're going to "add value" to their firm. "Stand out. You've got to get into that banana split area."

Maybe we are in the banana split area already, because sometimes things get too slippery even for Ron. On the subject of the "Five Achilles' Heels of a Career Search," one of which is "lack of focus," he launches into a meandering metaphor about being at a train station and deciding you might not want to get on the same train again. Or you might want to check out where the other trains are going, or you might get on your usual train and get off at another stop. Turning to values, he tells us, "Most successful candidates get in touch with their values." But what are values? "Values aren't the same as morals. Greed can be a value." Perhaps as a disclaimer, he tells us, "Males are not very good with the vision stuff."

But there's all sorts of useful information here too, which I struggle to commit to my notebook. Ask people to give you their contacts, and when they do, write them thank-you notes by hand, on nice stationery. Get a fountain pen; ballpoint won't do. If you can't get a real interview, at least ask for a twenty-minute "contact interview" aimed at prying contacts out of people. Wear a suit and tie or the female equivalent at all times, even on weekends, and Ron seems to give me a warning glance here; the sneakers have been noted. Network everywhere. One fellow "landed" thanks to networking at a

7-Eleven on a Saturday morning; luckily he had been fully
suited up at the time.

During a brief break devoted to restrooms and refilling our
plates, Paul catches me in the corridor and tells me his story
again, only in this version it was just yesterday, not a week ago,
when the boss warned him of the impending layoffs. I don't
think he's lying; I think that the boss's baleful speech has simply filled up Paul's brain and is occupying all the available time
slots in memory. He will get to tell the story yet again, since our
final hour is devoted to giving three-minute "commercials"—a
sort of long version of the "elevator speeches" Kimberly and
Joanne recommended. I listen in awe as my fellow seekers rise
from their seats to summarize careers spent managing
multimillion-dollar accounts, launching new products and
technologies, reviving dying enterprises. Not only am I wearing sneakers, but I seem to have passed through the world
without leaving a dent.

This time I am somewhat prepared, though I haven't memorized my speech and am counting on the presence of an audience to awaken the impulse to entertain. I say that PR and event
planning are very closely connected for me: my events make
news, and my press conferences are *events*. As for speechwriting, I don't mean to boast, but frankly I've found that events go
better if I write the major speeches. By prior decision, I hint at
successes that cannot be fully divulged due to confidentiality
agreements: as a PR person currently doing a lot of work with
celebrities, I say, I specialize in the hard cases where there are
drinking problems or anger management issues. The drinking-
problem idea had come up when Kimberly asked me to put my
career in something called "PAR" (Problem/Action/Results)

form. Once, on a book tour, my media escort had shared some dish about a certain well-known cookbook author who was inseparable from his fifth of vodka, and what a struggle it was to enforce coherency throughout a long day of back-to-back interviews. Kimberly felt this "problem" was unsuitable for a résumé, but it was the only one I could come up with. I pause to let my audience picture me deftly herding a series of drunk and disorderly celebrities, and conclude that I have always handled these cases with discretion, imagination, and cunning.

The word *cunning* seems to catch their attention, and I wonder if it's something I should use again. Donald suggests I do some networking through the PR professional association, which I have so far known only as a web site. Ron promises to e-mail me a contact.

Finally, it is Tim's turn to speak. He has not been just a run-of-the-mill HR guy; he's a union buster, though that's not his phrase. His résumé lists unions he has gone up against and defeated, and he stresses these victories in his "commercial." Neal, who has been largely silent since revealing his problems with getting up in the morning, asks Tim whether, if he can't find another HR job, he would consider working for labor instead. I mumble insincerely that Tim's experience might be really welcome at the AFL-CIO, right here in Washington. A beat goes by before Tim says, "Yes." Then he thinks for another few seconds, swallowing hard and blinking repeatedly, before saying, "Probably not. That would be a big adjustment."

So Tim has principles, which, under the circumstances, is almost shocking. No matter what the temptation, he'd remain loyal to the managerial class, just as, I suppose, Ron would reject an overture from the Democratic National Committee. I, on the other hand, have none. If Wyeth, the manufacturer of the hormone replacement drug that probably contributed to thousands of cases of breast cancer, offered me a job doing damage control in the press—well, under the terms of this project, I'd have to take it. But the way things are going, that is beginning to seem as unlikely as an AFL-CIO bid for Tim.

four

The Transformation

Ron instructed us to devise a "Winter-Spring Plan of Attack," and I find the military metaphor oddly reassuring. This is not just a matter of "attitude," or hope, or the projection of winning force fields; no, everything hinges on the cool logic of strategy. I will need a three-part plan, I decide, because in Western culture important things come in groups of three. Every public speaker knows this: two points are unconvincing; four are long-winded and superfluous; it takes exactly three to suggest roundedness and completion. And the first part of the plan is, once again, as emphasized by Ron, networking—sustained and furious, skilled and highly targeted, relentless and dogged.

My major takeaway from Ron, now that I have a chance to reflect, is that getting a job is like gaining acceptance into an eighth-grade clique. There exists an elite consisting of people who hold jobs and have the power to confer that status on others, and my task is to penetrate this elite. Since my actual eighth-grade status never advanced beyond that of loathsome pariah and nerd, I have no practical experience of elite crashing, but it makes sense to include a ruthless scrutiny of the "product" I am trying to sell. My résumé was finally judged "great" by Joanne, perhaps only because we ran out of sessions. It's the wrapping, so to speak—my physical appearance—that concerns me now. Sociologist Robert Jackall observes that in the world of corporate managers, "appearances—in the broadest sense—mean everything,"[1] and, if it is to keep up with the standards set by the résumé, mine needs a careful reevaluation.

Fortunately, I discover on the web, there are companies that will do this for me, and I call one of them, Image Management in Atlanta. The man who answers the phone asks whether I am interested in "body language or colors." Both, I say, the whole package, and am told it will cost $250 for a three-hour session. Call this part two of the Winter-Spring Plan of Attack: product enhancement.

But what about part three? An upgraded persona will not help without upgraded marketing methods, and to this end I read *Nonstop Networking* by Andrea R. Nierenberg, described in large print on the book jacket as "the Queen of Networking." The book seems to be addressed to the same market as the antidepressant that is advertised as a cure for "social anxiety." "Standing in the doorway," Nierenberg acknowledges, oblivious to the dangling participle, "a networking event can seem scary." The trick is to break the networking process down to "baby steps," such as "establish[ing] eye contact" and "ask[ing] an

---

1. Jackall, *Moral Mazes*, p. 59.

open-ended question." If you are still nervous, you can "use a script," rehearsing it "until it comes across naturally."[2]

Sample ice-breaking questions are offered: "Why did you come to this session? Where do you work and what do you do? Where do you live? What other sessions have you attended?"[3] I study the photo of Nierenberg on the book cover—the gray jacket and thick silver necklace, the dark lip gloss and the excessive eye shadow, which gives her a slightly loopy, half-asleep look—and imagine myself approaching her with the incisive question "What other sessions have you attended?"

I decide to go to Atlanta for a session at the image management firm and, it occurs to me as an afterthought, a follow-up visit to Patrick, who has indeed called, though I was not home at the time, to inquire as to what further coaching I might need. On the same trip, I will make use of any networking events I find advertised on the Atlanta Job Search Network. No more shyness or prideful reticence; I resolve to be a networking fool.

I make a reservation at the cheapest downtown hotel I can find, for an amazingly low $59 a night, secure a rental car, and pack every vaguely "professional" item of clothing I possess, which fortunately requires no more than a single small suitcase, even with the laptop thrown in. Just to be extra prepared, I spend one of my last nights at home watching Patrick's video, which I purchased at the boot camp, on how to find one's "career sweet spot." It is shockingly bad, so bad it begins to fill me with a zany self-confidence. Patrick is shown addressing a classroom in which about twenty adults are seated at desk

---

2. Andrea R. Nierenberg, *Nonstop Networking: How to Improve Your Life, Luck, and Career* (Sterling, VA: Capital Books, 2002), pp. 77, 78–79.
3. Ibid., p. 18.

chairs with their backs to the camera. He wanders through his spiel, holding my attention only when he embarks on an anecdote I had not heard before, about how he once had $1 million, and then, well—his gaze wanders from the camera to the wall—apparently it got away from him. Occasionally the action is interrupted by a screen containing a text message, generally in the form of three bulleted points. I give up in boredom halfway through, only later in the evening realizing that I am a PR person, and what Patrick desperately needs is *me*.

The plan takes form in my last day at home. Patrick will think I am coming for a coaching session, but I will in fact be coming to propose that he hire me himself. The best outcome would be that he does in fact hire me, and I exit the realm of the jobless just like that. In the second-best outcome, he will be sufficiently impressed to invite me to join his inner sanctum, the ExecuTable, in which he brings together the most promising of his job seekers with local business leaders. Or of course he could simply laugh me out of his office, but at least I would have gotten some valuable practice in "selling myself." So the Winter-Spring Plan of Attack now has the necessary troika of elements, which I list as Network, Change Self (that's the image enhancement part), and Sell Self. I cannot be sure, though, that the last two items are really separate and freestanding, since to "sell myself" I will need to transform myself into someone very different, psychologically speaking, from whatever I have been in my life up till now.

MY FIRST NETWORKING session in Atlanta is a major disappointment. I check into my hotel, noting that it is cheap for a reason—dingy and with the only available food being some

Stouffers frozen dinners in a freezer next to the registration desk. But at least I have a fridge and microwave, a TV, and a desk, plus there is a computer attached to a printer that guests can use in the lobby. It's still light when I drive out to the networking event venue, the Roasted Garlic restaurant in a northern suburb. This event, which came to me via the Atlanta Job Search Network, is sponsored by the congenially titled Layoff Lounge and aimed at the executive job seeker. Between the garlic and the lounging, I expect a convivial scene and possibly something decent to eat.

The Roasted Garlic occupies a site in a drab shopping center at which most of the stores are already closed for the night. It's one of those dark, suburban Italianate places, where most of the action centers on the bar. I am directed upstairs to a room packed with about thirty people seated around long tables facing the inevitable PowerPoint screen—a motley crowd, ranging in age from thirties to late fifties, mostly in studied business casual, and featuring a few black faces.

No networking occurs, however, except furtively and on the margins. Instead we are subjected to two hours of lectures accompanied by PowerPoint slides, and in case these fail to get the message across, we also are each given notebooks titled "Mastering Executive Job Change" and containing the same PowerPoint slides in paper form. Look up and you see

I. Managing Career Transition and Change Strategy
   A. Understanding Your Current Emotional Needs
   B. Gain Control

Look down and you see the very same thing, unless, of course, you have been flipping ahead. But it's probably just as well that our eyes are so fully engaged, since this is a sad, tacky place that we have come to, unenriched by even a whiff of the eponymous vegetable. Fake ivy on trellises lines the wall behind me, and I am facing a needlepoint rendition of a seaside town, possibly Italian, heavy on the burgundy and browns. Only a curtain keeps us from looking down on the bar scene on the main floor, but the curtain does nothing to dampen the familiar bar sounds of mumblings and the occasional squeal or hoot.

The content of the presentation attests to a major erosion of middle-class life: "Job change"—or, more accurately, job loss—has become inevitable, the speaker tells us, several times in a lifetime, and it is always accompanied by drastically straitened circumstances. How to manage? Much useful, but exhausting, information follows on preserving one's 401(k) plan, health insurance, and credit rating when the income ceases to flow, as well as a host of small tips: Raise some cash by holding a yard sale, and use the occasion to network with your neighbors. Cut the kids' allowances. Don't eat out and, when networking, arrange to meet for breakfast, not lunch, or better yet for coffee at Starbucks. "Every twenty dollars you can save," our speaker, a financial manager who resembles Alec Baldwin only without the sexual edge, tells us, "is a plank in the lifeboat you are building for yourself."

There are moments of bitter humor. On the subject of pensions, he asks, "You've heard of those?" to some slight snuffling sounds from the audience.[4] On health insurance, he says,

---

4. Pensions are becoming a thing of the past. In 1979, more than 80 percent of U.S. workers retired with a defined-benefit pension; by 2001, only a little over 40 percent did so. (Eduardo Porter and Mary Williams Walsh, "Retirement Turns into a Rest Stop as Pensions and Benefits Dwindle," *New York Times*, February 9, 2005.) As for health insurance, the health provisions of the Con-

"COBRA: It's not a snake, but it's going to seem like one when you see the quotes." The bright side, though, is that some trace of class privilege survives into the jobless condition. As executives, he reassures us, "instead of being laid off or out of work, we're 'in transition.'" This residual superiority can be deployed while asking the mortgage company for a few months' grace period. "You're executives here," the Baldwin lookalike declares, so you can go to the mortgage company without "your tail hanging between your legs."

We are given a break in which we are encouraged to order some food, despite the prohibition on eating out. This Roasted Garlic, the speaker tells us, is "the best-kept secret in Dunwoody." Having sampled a meal of tough chicken breast strips residing in a Campbell's soup–flavored sauce, I can report that it is a secret I can be counted on to keep. I chat with Leah Gray, the blond, thirtysomething woman sitting at my right, who shares my disappointment that this has not turned out to be a networking opportunity at all. No discussion has been built into the agenda, nor any time for the informal sharing of stories and tips.

Leah hands me a card that seems to be imprinted with a tiny résumé, in which most of the entries are undecipherable codes, like LINUX and SAP, and tells me she's been looking for another IT-related marketing job for six months now, going to events like this almost every weekday night. When I ask her what seem to be the most helpful events, she says there are a lot

---

solidated Omnibus Budget Reconciliation Act of 1986 (COBRA) allow laid-off workers from eligible firms to continue with their company's health insurance for eighteen months, if they pay 102 percent of the premiums. Because of these high costs, only about one in five unemployed workers utilizes the COBRA program (www.familiesusa.org.).

of things to go to, but that many of them are "very religious" and not particularly useful for contacts. At one networking event, she was challenged by one of the organizers to reveal where she is "churched," and walked out indignantly. She hastens to assure me there's nothing wrong with networking events being "religious"; it's just not what she goes to them for.

Not all of the scheduled networking events pan out. The night after the Roasted Garlic gathering, I head out for a networking meeting at a downtown Episcopal church, where a kindly female pastor informs me that the meeting time was changed and looks prepared to offer me a free meal and a place to sleep. I rush back to the hotel and do a Mapquest search for Congregation Beth Shalom, where the "Career Mavens" are said to be meeting, but I wouldn't get there till eight and the event ends at eight thirty. The next morning I'm up before six for the forty-five-minute drive out to a Golden Corral on the far west side, but the place isn't even open and a guy who's mopping the floor inside has no clue as to where the meeting might have migrated to.

Even with these gaps in the schedule, my home life, such as it is, is busy enough. Clothes have to be maintained in presentable condition. Food has to be procured, which turns out to be more of a challenge than you might expect at a "downtown" location. Within a two-block radius of the hotel, I can get a burger at Checkers or a larger one, with salad, at a sports-oriented pub. A great deal of time goes into planning my next outings with the help of Mapquest and two maps I have purchased, one small and laminated, one vast and impossible to read in the dim light of my room. I know I should be networking with every human form that presents itself—the wan Euro-tourists in the hotel, who may have confused Atlanta with

Atlantis or some other more seductive destination, the happy-hour clientele at the pub. But when the day is over, I want nothing so much as to pour myself a beer and shut down, alone in my room. How I earned the *E* for extrovert in my Myers-Briggs personality type is a mystery that only deepens.

IMAGE MANAGEMENT TURNS out to be located in a loft in what looks like a gentrified warehouse. I am greeted by Prescott, suavely outfitted in suit and tie, and introduced to his partner—a young Argentinian, as it emerges, who is dressed, more reassuringly, in nondescript urban casual. I barely get a chance to scan the loft space before being ushered into the windowless consultation room, but I note that it's done up in boas and third-world crafts and practically screams *Pride!* I'm hoping their image-managing sensibilities are as gay as their interior decorating tastes—because gays have been practicing at "passing" for decades, and that is pretty much my current assignment.

Robert Jackall's book impressed on me that corporate dress serves a far more important function than mere body covering. "Proper management of one's external appearances," he writes, "simply signals to one's superiors that one is prepared to undertake other kinds of self-adaptation."[5] By dressing correctly, right down to the accessories, you let it be known that you are willing to conform in other ways too—that you can follow orders, for example, and blend in with the prevailing "culture." But first I have to know what I am conforming to.

Naturally, I have already read a couple of dress-for-success

5. Jackall, *Moral Mazes*, p. 47.

books and learned that the idea is to pass as a hereditary member of the upper-middle class. As the leading expert in the field, John T. Molloy, puts it in his *New Women's Dress for Success*, "The executive suite is an upper-socioeconomic business club, and in order to get in you must wear the club uniform." [6] He advises a kind of preshopping ritual, in which you first scout out the expensive shops for clues as to appropriate textures and shapes, and only then repair to a more affordable setting for your actual purchases. I think I have the class thing pretty well in hand—muted colors, patternless fabrics, and natural fibers, for example—but my observations come largely from the academic and publishing worlds, which permit a dangerously wide latitude for personal expression in the form of flowing scarves, rumpled linen, and dangly earrings.

Then there is the vexing business of gender. All of the books warn that it's a lot trickier for a woman to pass than it is for a man, in part because the female "uniform" is not yet as standardized as a man's, so it's easier for a woman to go wrong. But the problem seems to go deeper than that, to the very biological underpinnings of gender: the features that make a man sexually attractive—handsomeness, tallness, a deep voice, et cetera— also work in his favor at the office, while female sexual attractiveness can torpedo a woman's career. Shoulder-length hair, an overly generous display of legs, or a "too busty" chest[7] can all undermine a woman's credibility. Beauty itself is a handicap.

Very beautiful young women have difficulty being taken seriously, especially by men, most of whom refuse to even think of

6. John T. Molloy, *New Women's Dress for Success* (New York: Warner Books, 1996), p. 16.
7. Ibid., p. 43.

them as experts or authority figures. In addition, beautiful women are seen by both sexes as lacking in intelligence—or at least as lightweights.[8]

I know I have no problem in the area of "too sexy," "too busty," or distractingly beautiful, but it is clear that for any woman, of any age or condition, being female is something to compensate for.[9]

While Prescott fetches some coffee for us from the kitchen, I try to skim through the purple-covered notebook he handed me, titled "The Personal Image Enhancement Program for [and the last two words are handwritten] Barbara Alexander." I'm distracted by the curious gizmo on the corner table separating our chairs, in which four small burning candles share space with an actual running water fountain, but I force myself to read, finding on page 1: "What motivates you to image-manage!" Not a question but answered anyway, sort of:

Your **exposure** in the marketplace, your **dependency** upon others to be successful and how often you come in **contact** with those dependencies, are three reasons why you should be motivated to develop and maintain a professional presence.

Fair enough, since I have entered a world where people seem to be judged not only by performance but by "image," and, the

8. Molloy, *New Women's Dress for Success*, p. 175.
9. In 1992, the *Washington Post* quoted Harvey Hornstein, a psychology professor at Columbia University who studies gender roles, as saying: "For women, it's a Catch-22. If they dress in 'feminine' ways, men don't think they're suited for the job. If women don't play the stereotypical role, then men complain they're not 'feminine' enough." (Amanda Spake, "Dressing for Power," *Washington Post*, January 5, 1992.)

notebook states ominously, "You need to understand that you are in total control of the images others form of you."

Just as I would prepare for a visit to the dental hygienist with extra brushing and flossing, I have put unusual effort into my appearance today: mascara as well as eyeliner, lipstick enhanced with gloss, jacket and slacks, tailored pink shirt, and a muted gray silk scarf. Only now, as I await Prescott's return—I can hear him taking a phone call in the other room—are the multiple defects in my ensemble emerging. My pant socks, which I had taken to be black in the gloom of the hotel room, are actually navy blue, although my jacket is black. My watch cost $19 fifteen years ago, and the band no longer matches the face. Then there is the problem of the slacks: everything else is Ann Taylor, drastically reduced of course, but the slacks come from the sale rack at the Gap, and, as I see for the first time, the zipper does not go all the way up. If I were wearing a pullover, as I usually do, this wouldn't matter, but this shirt has to be tucked in. And what about the shoes, which are drably flat, and the "pearl" earrings, which I got at three for $10 at the Miami airport?

When Prescott returns with the coffee, I lay out the situation. I have been "consulting" for several years now and need to reconfigure myself for the corporate world, but have only the vaguest idea of how to proceed. Plus, I throw in, though I didn't plan to, I'm concerned that I make no visual impression at all. This impression—an impression of an impression, really—stems from a newspaper profile of me some years ago, in which I was described as the kind of person whom no one would notice when she enters a room. At the time that had seemed like good news; at least I had figured out how to blend in. But now I need to leave some sort of memory trace in the people I meet. Prescott nods approvingly and congratulates me for coming to him: "Some job seekers neglect the visuals."

Furthermore, I confide, my exposure to corporate dress comes mostly from New York and San Francisco, where a black-based minimalism still prevails, whereas here in Atlanta, you see a lot of bright red accented with gold. He confirms this, adding that not only are there regional differences in corporate costuming, so are there differences from company to company. Some are extremely conservative; others he calls "corporate creative." It is wise to know what the rules are before showing up for the interview, because you do, after all, want to look like a "team player," right down to the team uniform. To find out what is expected, study any photographs of female executives you can find on the company web site or call and ask a receptionist to tell you what the power gals are wearing—unless, of course, it occurs to me, the receptionist hates the power gals and maliciously advises me to show up in harem pants and bustier.

Now we proceed to the material at hand, which is me. As in so many of my coaching experiences, we begin by categorizing me as a "type," only here no test is involved, only a quick all-over survey by Prescott. I am "angular" in shape, he announces, and my face is shaped "like a diamond," which suggests to me a pointy head, but in fact refers to my cheekbones. They are "wonderful"; I can keep them. My hair and even the $3 earrings pass muster; they can stay too. As for my overall type, there are four possibilities: "classic," which applies to people who always wear skirts, "are not very flexible, and tend to be Republican"; "romantic," who "love flowing material"; "dramatic," who "love to break rules" and are often "eccentric"; and "natural," who are "outdoorsy, want to save owls and trees, love texture, and don't wear a lot of patterns." I turn out to be a natural, which seems to please Prescott, because "there's less to change." Fashion-wise, I am a kind of tabula rasa.

The first problem is that I come across as "too authoritative" as a result of the combination of an "angular" body with a tailored shirt and the straight lines of my jacket lapel. "You want to look *approachable,* not authoritative, so people will feel comfortable working with you," and this means curved lines, not straight ones.

Decoding this diagnosis, I see that I am not looking feminine enough.[10] This is, to say the least, confusing. The dress-for-success books all urge what I take to be a somewhat mannish appearance, achieved through pragmatic hairstyles and curve-concealing suits. But if you go too far in the masculine direction, Prescott is saying, you somehow err again. What could be threatening about a tailored shirt? I recall, from my other life as an amateur historian, that subordinated people often used imitation as a form of mockery; some nineteenth-century colonized Africans and enslaved black Caribbeans, for example, liked to strut around on festive occasions in the full regalia of British officers. Maybe an overly masculine office outfit on a woman sends the same kind of signal—as a sly mockery of the male-dominated corporate hierarchy.

---

10. Marcia Clark, the prosecutor in O. J. Simpson's murder trial, was given a similar diagnosis. According to the *Chicago Tribune,* "After a focus group assembled by a jury consultant criticized her appearance and manner of presentation, Clark has changed her highly successful style. She has changed her hairstyle, dress and personal manner, become softer, more feminine, warmer and more open—in short, less like the aggressive trial lawyer she is and more like a stereotypical woman." (Cynthia Grant Bowman, "Fashion Weighs in on Simpson Case," *Chicago Tribune,* October 30, 1994.)

"As for body language," Prescott continues, "the way you're holding your hands on your waist, you seem to be holding something in."

This is true. I release one hand and send it over to pick up the coffee cup. But the other one must remain at its post, covering the gap in my zipper.

"There needs to be a necklace to pull it all together," he goes on.

I protest that, with glasses, earrings, scarf, and brooch all vying for attention in the head and chest region, a necklace could be overkill. But no, a necklace will apparently be a peacemaker, not an additional contender.

The recitation of flaws continues, almost faster than I can write them down. There's the issue of suits: you cannot wear slacks with nonmatching jackets. The top and bottom must form a single unit, perhaps the better to resemble a military uniform. Charitably, he says nothing about the watch, just gently suggests that I go for a larger watch face, preferably with a gold band.

He moves along to color in general, where I receive a major blow: I can never wear gray or black again, because they drain the color from my face. This pretty much condemns me to nudity, since my entire wardrobe is black and gray, and not because I'm striving for New York City–style coolness, circa 1995. The truth is I spill on everything, so no peach or yellow item has ever survived more than two or three wearings. Even my conservative silver brooch, a gift from my Norwegian publisher, is deemed "not corporate" by Prescott. All this time I had thought I was a perfectly presentable-looking middle-class professional, when in fact I must come across as a misfit, a mess.

If Prescott wasn't so perfect—so perfectly groomed, so perfectly discreet—this might be unbearable. I have plenty of excuses to offer, but of course I do not inflict them on him. Mainly, as a writer, I have no need to dress for work in anything other than gym clothes, or no clothes at all for that matter, and when writers do try to "dress up," they are generally granted a lot of leeway. I remember attending a banquet with the poet and short-story writer Grace Paley, who appeared in a loose pink floral dress. When I complimented her, she confessed it was a nightgown, which was obvious on closer inspection.

Finished with the assessment, Prescott leads me off to a second small, windowless room, where we sit at a counter facing a mirror to address the matter of cosmetics. He asks to see my current collection, so I am forced to display the contents of my makeup kit, as if this were an airline security check: two lipsticks, a tinted moisturizer, pressed powder, blush, mascara, and eyeliner. "*Liquid* eyeliner?" Yes, incredibly enough. Most of this must be tossed: The lipsticks contain hidden grays that are dragging me down; the blush is another carrier of lethal gray. The pressed powder, I am mortified to report, presents a slightly ridged surface that he identifies as a bacterial colony fed by oils from my skin. So all this time I have been patting my face with microbial scum. I can see that I am in for an additional splurge on his special line of makeup in addition to the $250 for our session.

After I am deftly—and rather well, I must say—made up with his own concoctions, he places a kind of bolero consisting of layers of different color swatches around my neck, turning one over at a time, so that I appear to be dressed sequentially in brown, yellow, green, red, orange, peach, et cetera. "See that," he says, turning to a forbidden hue—"how it's making you pasty?" I agree that I resemble a cave dweller or corpse. Then he shows me a "good" color and insists that I acknowledge the rich, honey tones it imparts to my face. I again agree, although as far as I can see, I still look faintly tubercular.

This should be the fun part—playing with paints and little swatches of fabric—but I am suddenly gripped by queasiness. I understand that to make myself into a "product" that I can market, I must first become a commodity, a thing. I further understand that the queasiness may simply be a follow-up to the Checkers' bacon double cheeseburger I had for lunch. But there is an unmistakable pallor shining through the professional makeup job. What I had not understood is that to become an object, a thing, you must first go through a kind of death.

I make some excuse about a four o'clock appointment and buy $55.50 worth of cosmetics with the assurance I can always order more of Prescott's personal selections by e-mail. I get to keep my own mascara. Then I head back to the hotel, park, and start walking aimlessly past office towers and happy-hour joints, through nondescript neighborhoods and downtown parks, until the paint comes off my face in the rain.

THE NEXT AFTERNOON I drive an hour or so outside of Atlanta to see Patrick. His office turns out to be in a shopping center anchored by a Kinko's and a Chick-Fil-A, where I prime myself with an iced tea. I am dressed in the same clothes I wore for my image makeover, having refreshed the shirt by washing out the armpit areas in the sink and drying them with the blow-dryer, and I've memorized my major talking points: why he needs me, what I can offer, the bright future ahead. This strategy is based on the advice books, which urge you to research the prospective employer thoroughly in advance, then to use the interview—not to prattle on about yourself but to talk about what you can do for the company. Jeffrey J. Fox's canny book *Don't Send a Resume*, for example, explains encouragingly that "the company may not know it needs you"—until, that is, you outline "five or six ways the company could be improved."[11] Hydraulic fluid leaks? Overly long shipment times? You point out these defects and explain how you'll fix them.

But something has gone badly wrong with the plan, I see as soon as I enter his office, which is located right above a Chinese take-out place. I envisioned an office *suite,* staffed at least by a receptionist, and containing a sort of boardroom where the ExecuTable insiders would gather periodically for coffee and croissants. But Patrick opens the door himself, revealing a room the size of a walk-in closet. He seems to have deteriorated significantly from the voluble guru of boot camp. He's wearing a sweatshirt and jeans, as if in conscious defiance of corporate propriety, and has the puffy, pained look of a man who's been recently boiled.

When I am seated on the couch, he inquires as to the status of my search. For a moment, I am almost too overwhelmed by the death-of-a-salesman vibe to respond. I should make some excuse and flee. I should admit to even greater "obstacles" than I had revealed at the boot camp and submit to a normal coaching session. It doesn't look to me as if he could afford to hire even a cleaning lady, not that such a person would find any clear surfaces to clean here anyway, what with the clutter of pop-psych and self-improvement books stashed on the desk

11. Fox, *Don't Send a Resume*, pp. 33–35.

and rising from the floor. But I am programmed to proceed and cannot deviate from the Plan. In the spirit of a person who has walked to the end of the plank and is taking her first steps out onto air, I announce, "Patrick, I've been thinking about it. I've studied your video and my notes from the boot camp, and I think *you* should hire me. You need a PR person. You need an image makeover. And I'm the person to do it."

Getting no response except for a sudden neck twitch that seems to be addressed to a muscle pain, I plunge into my prepared pitch: The career coaching industry can only expand. Whether or not the economy improves. And this is because the corporate world has changed. Today, in the wake of the last recession, companies are intent on being permanently lean; they churn people in and out as needed, so that the average executive or professional can expect to hold—what?—about ten or eleven jobs in a lifetime whether he or she wants to or not.[12] And it's interesting, isn't it, that our society is so unprepared for this change. College, for example, prepares people for jobs, but not for the trauma of job change. Hence the huge long-term market for career coaching, which Patrick is poised to conquer. There's big money to be made. Very big.

"I was the first career coach," he interjects tonelessly. "I started in the seventies, before all the rest of them came along."

"Fine." Now I think I have him where I want him. He's accepting my framework for this event, or at least he's not imposing his own, and this gives me the courage to rattle on: You have a gift. Anyone can see that. Many things can be learned, but the way he works with people, which I saw at the boot

12. Sennett, *The Corrosion of Character*, p. 22.

camp, that's not something that can be learned. The ability to look at a person and really see what's going on with them. When I watched him at the boot camp, I couldn't believe he wasn't a trained psychotherapist.

"Well, I am. I've done that."

The flattery is working, and—who knows?—there is an outside possibility that he might be able to raise the money to hire me from some of his executive contacts. But you're more than a psychotherapist, I continue, "because you can galvanize a whole group at the same time. That's called charisma. That's something you have or you don't. You're born with that. It comes from inside."

"I know," he says, addressing the bookshelf. "I have a gift."

"The thing is, Patrick," I say as gently as possible, "you're *stuck*." That's his word and his central theme in the "sweet spot" video—dealing with people who are stuck.

"Like look at that boot camp," I continue. "Now I don't know what your plan is, your mission, and if you want to tell me it's to reach the laid-off sixty-five-K-a-year middle manager, fine, I have complete respect for that. It's an important demographic, and I can respect you if your mission is to work with them. I admire you for that." I am trying to suggest that his operation might as well be the Salvation Army, and he is twisting his neck again, so all I can see is the corner of his eyes.

"But," I go on, "that's not where the money is. If you're looking to make money, you have to aim for the one- to two-hundred-K person. And that's where I can help you."

"But we're here to talk about Barbara Alexander," he says, tapping the legal pad on his lap.

"We are. We're talking about what she can do for you." I

have never before in my life spoken of myself in the third person, but then this emerging Barbara Alexander person is not exactly myself, or anyone I would want to know. Maybe the makeover is kicking in, or maybe it's Patrick's own philosophy, which I acquired at boot camp: *EP* varies exponentially with *PSWB*, meaning that my inner self-confidence can bend the world to my will. Clearly thrown off, he gets up and moves to the desk chair, as if to reabsorb his lost authority through the seat of his pants.

"Let's talk about your video, the one about the sweet spot. It doesn't work. Terrible production values. And look at the *semiotics* of it—that's a word we use in PR," I tell him, amazed at my own creativity. "You've got a bunch of people that you're supposedly interacting with, inspiring, and all we see is the backs of their heads."

"I only had one camera."

I shrug. "Why didn't you invest more in something so important?"

"But there was great energy in the room."

"Maybe, but the viewer doesn't see it. They don't get a hint of your charisma."

Since he seems to accept this, I plunge deeper. What else is there to do, now that I've started, except to see the plan through? "The other thing is that I do coaching on public speaking. You're very, very good, but you could be better. Trouble is, you tend to flub your anecdotes; you let them dribble away; you don't draw the point. I can help with that. You need a crisper approach."

"So . . . you . . . want," he says, letting each syllable struggle to find its way out, "to . . . market . . . me."

If it weren't for the sepulchral tone of this utterance, I might be annoyed. Where has he been for the past twenty minutes? But it's clear I'm not just dealing with a severe case of narcissism here. Right before my eyes, a man is being sucked down into some dark sticky substrate of the mind. I want to save him. I also—where is this coming from?—want to push him down deeper into the enveloping muck. "Listen to yourself," I say, leaning forward, "how your voice falls when you say that. What I'm picking up on here is depression."

If he can be a psychotherapist, so can I. If he could reduce Cynthia to tears with a diagnosis, I can offer one of my own. At any moment, of course, he's free to say, "Look, I'll do the coaching here, thank you very much," and crush my chutzpah under his heel.

"It's the sleeping pills I'm taking; they make me like this."

Aha, further vulnerability! I have the sense now of being engaged in a life-or-death struggle; whose grift will prevail? I return to my qualifications as a PR person, the brilliant nationwide successes, the careers I have helped launch. He could still win if he could find the strength to patronize me, as in: "That's great, now I want you to go out and try this on a real potential employer"—perhaps accompanied by an indulgent chuckle. But no, he has to get defensive: "You haven't seen anything of my true gifts," he says, "just this much"—indicating the tip of his pinky.

I acknowledge my ignorance as to the true extent of his gifts.

"You're saying a lot of things, but you don't know what I've been going through recently," he says, and moves on to a list of explanations that would be laughed out of his own boot camp as "excuses." There was a "business divorce" involving a sudden loss of assets. He had to find another apartment and move to this smaller office. Three long-term clients unexpectedly bailed. As for the boot camp, with its population of $65K guys, that was not typical for him. He just "cherry-picks" the boot camps to get people for his ExecuTable. That's where he makes his real money.

Inspired by his own defense, he makes another attempt to seize power: "But you're here for some coaching, right?"

I could be really mean. I could demand to know, "What's Patrick's problem?" and shout "Patrick!" as the boot campers did with the hapless Kevin. But I just barrel along with my plan for him. In the boot camp he had mentioned that he is writing a book, I remind him. That could be the platform we launch him from. When will it be done? Because with the book in hand . . . And I outline the book tour, the Oprah appearance, the lecture bookings, and how about a Wall Street event—a lunch maybe, for some of the movers and shakers, with him as the speaker?

"You could do that?"

I assure him that I do that and more every day of my life as a PR person-slash-event planner. Could he give me a brief summary of the book?

This, it seems to me, is his last chance to rise from the mat and reclaim his position as coach. But he seems to have lost interest in the match, or maybe I never quite engaged his attention. "If a person has a gift . . . ," he begins, and goes off into a couple of sentences that are too garbled for me to record in my notes.

Hmmm, we're not quite there yet, I tell him, but not to worry; it's almost as much effort to perfect a media-ready summary as it is to write the book itself. Plus, I can help him write the book. I can edit, pull things together. Does he have a publisher? No. An agent? No. I can help him with all that. I'm connected.

The hour is coming to an end, thank God, and I want to be the first to acknowledge this fact. I tell him that I don't want to take up any more of his time, although it is hard to imagine that he has anything else to do with it, the phone having rung only once during our time together—a low rate of interpersonal contact, I cannot help but observe, for the self-proclaimed inventor of career coaching. One of the things I learned from Kimberly is to tell people exactly what you want them to do for you, so I tell him two things: First, I want him to think my proposition over. I know it must be strange, coming out of the blue like this, but I'm perfectly serious. Second, I want him to let me into the ExecuTable group.

He has one last bit of fight in him. As I pack away my notebook and pen, he announces that he could coach me on "presentation." My manner is too "gruff."

Gruff? It seems to me an odd word to apply to a person who has spent the last hour cajoling, persuading, *selling.*

"You told me all kinds of things without knowing what I'm going through. You seem *angry.*"

I am taken aback. I don't feel any anger toward Patrick— pity, of course, and a certain contempt for his entire profession. If I'm guilty of anything here, it is an excess of that vaunted corporate quality—*focus.* I came to sell myself and did not let myself get deflected from this mission by Patrick's obvious distress; wicked from a humane point of view, perhaps, but perfectly acceptable, I had thought, for a go-getting, proactive, highly focused, "seasoned professional." Yes, I've been using a beaten man to hone my self-selling skills, but Kimberly, I suspect, would approve.

Then too—how could I have forgotten?—I'm a woman. The typically masculine word *gruff* is the clue that I have broken some perhaps Atlanta-based gender rule here. Maybe it's the "inaccessible" tailored shirt. But I do not give an inch. It's not anger, I say, it's aggressiveness, and I apologize if I was too direct but I'd do the same in any potential employment situation: tell the interviewers exactly why they need me and what I can do for them.

"Well, you haven't told me anything I don't already know."

"Good, people only really hear what they already know." With that brilliant riposte, I offer to pay him for his time, since I've taken up an hour that could have been used as a coaching session. He says the fee will be $175, quite a bit more than the $75 he mentioned in his e-mail confirmation of our session, but I write the check without comment, shake his hand, remind him I'll be calling in a week, and leave.

So who won? If a job was the goal, I lost, but I knew from the moment I entered his office that there was no job to be had. The important thing, I tell myself, is that I managed to make my pitch for almost an hour, and this man supposedly gifted with such superior insight, such rare "people skills," never saw through it. Unless you count that outburst of sexist cattiness at the very end, he was taken in, even tempted, by visions of Oprah dancing before his eyes. On the other hand, he's the one who has the $175, so from a brutal bottom-line perspective, he's the one who came out ahead.

I make my way back down the freeway toward the hotel, aware of all the feelings appropriate to a pacifist on the occasion of his first kill. Yes, I am filled with self-loathing and disgust.

Slime oozes from my hands onto the steering wheel; the white noise of the road is filled with muffled denunciations and curses brought down on my soul. But I did it, didn't I? I tried selling myself, and for an hourlong stretch I wasn't half bad. I have blooded my sword.

five

Networking
with the Lord

I come home to the realization that my trip, which cost me more than $1,000, airfare included, netted me little more than a lip pencil, a tube of foundation, and a handful of business cards. In fact, I am almost four months into my search—a point at which I expected to be running from interview to interview. The daffodils are fighting their way up in my tiny front yard and my cash reserves have sunk by almost $4,000, but I am not noticeably any closer to employment than when I started back in December.

I have applied to at least fifty pharmaceutical and health-related companies and, following Kimberly's advice, have even begun proactively approaching companies where no appropriate jobs are posted. For example, I leap on a start-up called Extend Fertility, which was brought to my attention by a fellow journalist in a context unrelated to my job search. For a considerable price, the company offers to freeze women's eggs for implantation at a convenient, but reproductively over-the-hill phase of life. My cover letter to this firm enthuses over its mission and my extensive experience with women's health issues. I follow up with more e-mails and a phone call—only to be told that ExtendFertility doesn't need a PR person just now. Again playing the feminist card, I discover and apply to a company called Frank About Women, which is "dedicated to helping companies create enriching and enduring brand relationships with women," but to no effect.

On the darker side, I approach a "neuromarketing" firm called Brighthouse, which I find listed in an article called "The Ten Worst Corporations in America"—its aim being to apply neurological research to advertising, bypassing the conscious mind to appeal directly to the brain's pleasure centers. Obviously, whether the folks of Brighthouse know it or not, they need my help. The beginning of my cover letter has an extortionary ring:

> A recent article posted at zmag.org lists Brighthouse as one of the "ten worst corporations in America." You may want to ignore the slur, which, in my reading, was highly ideologically slanted against the kind of neurological research you are involved in.
>
> Or you might want to reevaluate your public relations strategy.

But this fails to strike fear into their hearts; nor do any of the Brighthouse functionaries whose names I track down on the web bother to take my phone calls.

Aside from my cybersearching, the only thing to do is to keep on networking—more intensively, though, and in repackaged form. If I learned one big lesson from my encounters with Prescott and Patrick, it is that I have to become softer, more feminine, and "approachable." So I head for Ann Taylor in the mall two miles from home, which I trust to know far more about the corporate look than I do, and zone in immediately on a tan—not black—pants suit with an accessibly curved, rather than straight-lined, lapel, which is on sale at half price, about $160. Our local department store supplies $15 gold earrings, and although I know there should be a gold necklace "to pull it all together," none comes to my attention. The message should be more like what Prescott recommended: approach me, please, I'm perfectly harmless.

But where to network? The answer has already come to me in a curious way. At Patrick's boot camp, I was heading for the bathroom on one of our breaks when I was intercepted by a short man whose head formed a perfect triangle from pointy bald pate to lushly padded jowls. He was a successful graduate of Patrick's individual coaching program, who had moved from a corporate layoff to managing a fried chicken franchise. "If you're looking for places to network," he said, "you'll want to go to Godel.com," and he wrote the URL on the back of his business card.

For a moment I reeled, feeling like a character in an early Pynchon novel who has just been handed a major clue in a plot that will never be resolved, that will only grow in ever-proliferating complexity. Every science nut is aware of Godel's Theorem, which states that no mathematical system can ever be both consistent and complete. It's a kind of postmodernist warning—just when you think you've got everything sewed up into one beautiful theory, you'll find you've left something out—and has always filled me with a thick sense of defeat. I thanked my informant as warmly as I could and stuffed his card in my pocket.

Now at home I come across the card when I am preparing to wash my slacks. The home page of the Godel web site features a brief tribute to our troops in Iraq, and in a few clicks I come to a calendar in which every day, weekends excepted, is filled with regularly scheduled networking events for the Atlanta job searcher. On most days you can find a 7:30 or 8:00 A.M. breakfast meeting at a Shoney's or some similar venue as well as a lunch meeting and an evening get-together in an area church. Here it is, laid out for me. There is no escape from another bout with Atlanta.

BACK AT MY $59-a-night hotel, I decide to confirm my first networking destination before setting off on another wild-goose chase through the suburbs. No phone numbers for the various networking groups are listed on the Godel web site, so I call the Godel accounting firm, which is listed, and am soon talking to Mr. Laimon Godel himself. He apologizes for the web site's deficiencies and boomingly invites me to "a real networking event"—a lunch meeting tomorrow—where I'll be mingling with the local business community and no doubt collect a handful of leads. In fact, he says, "You can come as my guest." I take this as a real networking triumph on my part, or at least evidence of a winning telephone manner.

The site of the Norcross Fellowship Lunch is a suburban Shoney's just off the highway, where the restaurant host ushers me into a side room labeled "NFL." "Is this the National Football League?" I inquire gaily of a gray-haired fellow who is so far the sole other occupant of the room. No response; he must have heard that one a few times before. So I try again, more soberly, with my name and mission: relocating to Atlanta, seeking a job. This at least elicits his name, Larry, and the information that he owns a car wash.

"Would you be needing a public relations person?" I inquire, trying to regain my come-hither tone. The narrow look he gives me raises the possibility that there's something off-color about "public relations," maybe the "relations" part. Or it could be my outfit, which may be too dressy, given that Larry has come in good-old-boy casual. But I am saved by the arrival of another, more outgoing, Larry, who suggests we move on to fill our plates at the buffet. We all do, and I am struck by the first Larry's choices: a mound of lettuce, covered with canned fruit salad, topped by a desiccated gray hamburger patty and dripping with Thousand Island dressing.

Now the chairs, which are arranged at long tables facing in the direction of the buffet, are filling up, mostly with white men, but there are a handful of women—none of them wearing even a splash of black. I try a conversation with Mac, an older man who is sitting next to car-wash Larry, and is introduced to me as an author. "What have you written?" I ask, and he hands me a thin, pamphlet-sized volume titled *Mega Values: 10 Global Principles for Business and Professional Success— WRITTEN IN STONE*. The ten principles, he explains, are the Ten Commandments, which he has translated into practical guidelines for businesspeople.

As Mac turns away to greet new arrivals, I open the book and discover that the first commandment—"You shall have no other gods before Me"—is rendered as "Show proper respect for authority," such as one's boss. This would seem to contradict the original, since the secular authorities may not always

be in tune with God, may in fact be serving the false god
Mammon.

With Mac engaged and the dour Larry occupied with his
hamburger salad, I turn to the fellow sitting to my right, who
looks noticeably more upper-middle-class than most of the
crowd—an IT specialist, it turns out, who also runs a weekly
morning session for job seekers. Any tips for me? He tells me
to study the local business newspaper and, echoing Kimberly,
to avoid wasting time with my fellow job seekers. Surprisingly,
he also advises against using career coaches—"there are plenty
of free sources of information."

"You mean on the Internet?"

"Mmm," he says, without elaborating.

"Why is it almost all men here?" I venture to ask.

"Most of these groups started out all male. It's a religious
thing."

I want to ask what religion this might be, but settle for a
coy "You're sure it's OK for me to be here?" I am wishing my
"host," Mr. Godel, would show up and somehow identify
himself.

"Oh yeah, anyone can come now. And for you, it's a perfect place to network. You've got a lot of the real business
leaders here."

He returns to chewing, but the word *network* reminds me
of the advice in *NonStop Networking* to keep the conversation
going with some item from the news. "So, uh, has the outsourcing of IT to India had any effect on you?"

"No, and I think it's a good thing too. Let the Indians do the
easy stuff. Americans should be learning to do something new."

I cannot think of a response that will fall within the accessibly feminine framework I have set for myself, so I make do

with an appreciative "hmmm" and ask him if he would recognize Laimon Godel. "Over there," he says, and points out a round-faced fellow who is back-slapping his way around the room. I rise to introduce myself to Laimon, but the get-together suddenly comes to an official start with the affable Larry, who is introduced as the owner and operator of several mobile home parks, going to the lectern and shouting, "Praise the Lord!"

This exhortation is echoed by several people among the about fifty now assembled in the room, along with "amens." "We've been meeting for fifteen years now," Larry goes on, "and I know God's been present every time because scripture says wherever two or more of my followers meet, there am I." Now a man in a boldly striped sweater steps forward to give a blessing, which includes a request for prayers for an Atlantan who has gone to work as a missionary in Czechoslovakia—a country, I cannot help but note, that hasn't existed since 1993. Well, wherever the missionary has gone off to, a large white-haired man in the audience raises his right hand, palm to ceiling, and shuts his eyes in a gesture of prayer.

The fellow in charge of the blessing goes off into a long, meandering anecdote about a dying man, a doctor, and a dog, which is attributed to the last e-mail sent by "coach Venable" on his deathbed. As far as I can tell, the message is that we have nothing to fear from death, but I cannot be sure, since this is one extremely shaggy dog. Larry reclaims the lectern and, to my complete surprise, launches into the most incendiary part of the New Testament, the part about the rich man and the eye of the needle. Will the meeting come to a sudden end as everyone empties their pockets and rushes out to minister to the poor?

No, the point seems to be that the disciples were "afraid of what they might have to give up" and that Jesus taught them that they didn't have to give up all that much after all. "Praise the Lord!" concludes Larry.

Maybe I should have guessed from the word *fellowship,* although that had sounded pleasantly secular, as in "fellowship of the ring." But here it is, right on the blue sheet of paper that serves as a program: the "mission" of the NFL is to "provide a platform for Christian businessmen to share their story of how God has touched their lives both personally and professionally." Awkwardly enough, I am sitting in what is now the front of the gathering, just in front and a little to the side of the lectern, where any inappropriate facial expression could be visible to a good half of the assemblage. As for leaving—say, with a quick glance at my watch as if recalling some simultaneous appointment—that could only be interpreted as a statement, and surely a heretical one.

Besides, we have come to the moment for new people, like myself, to stand and introduce themselves. I give my name and the information that I am considering relocating to Atlanta and am looking for a PR job. A handful of other job seekers identify themselves and their desired jobs—chiefly in accounting and IT—though most of the new arrivals are established businessmen. A man in suit and tie gets applause for his announced intention to set up a similar fellowship for downtown lawyers—a mission no less risky than proselytizing in darkest Czechoslovakia to judge from the "oohs" and "ahs," which are mixed with a few jeers at the very notion of lawyers. Back to Larry, who has "just a few more words." "What a mixed-up world!" he observes, "where we can have a debate over whether a man can marry another man [chuckles from the audience] . . . Where we have a presidential candidate who says we shouldn't be over there [I assume he means in Iraq]. Whaddya do with people like that?"

There is an expectant silence as he scans the room before answering his own question: "Whip 'em!" Somehow the prospect of a whipping gets him going into a digression about how maybe it isn't politically correct to say that, because there are people today who want to tell you that you can't discipline your own children, but in some cases that's what you've got to do—whip 'em. This sets off general laughter and some self-satisfied buzz, enhanced by Mac, who calls out, "*Whup* 'em, as we say in the South!" to hearty applause.

What would Jesus do?—rise up and denounce the folksy sadism advocated in his name? I settle for a stony-faced silence, not that I have much choice without making a scene. Anyway, now that we are all presumably feeling cozy and bonded, it's time for the speaker, John D. Wise, whom Larry introduces as a real estate broker and "recovering attorney." Wise is a tall, strikingly handsome, white-haired guy in a visibly expensive suit, leading me to anticipate a polished delivery on the subject of real estate opportunities. He begins by asking God to give him the words he will need, but sadly this prayer goes largely ignored. In a stumbling manner, and with reference to a large number of handwritten sheets of paper in different sizes and colors, he sets out to narrate "three ways God's been working in my life." The first has to do with his conversion experience in 1981, when he was "moved to get on [his] knees and accept God." Such humility does not come easily to him, on account of his being a Texan. "Being from Texas is like being born red-haired, bald, or Jewish. Everybody notices, and you never grow out of it." The audience chuckles at this apparent witticism.

The next way God worked in Wise's life had to do with his wife, Laurie. One day she called him at work and told him she was frightened because there were four gypsies in the backyard, so he got in his car and raced home. "Look," she said, pointing out the window toward the edge of the woods, and she directed his attention to a gypsy wearing a red hat and another one, a little girl, in a yellow dress. Now he has everyone's breathless attention. "But you know what?" Wise asks. "*There was no one there.*"

It turns out that Laurie was suffering from delirium tremens, consequent on a brief drying out required for some minor surgery. We have already learned that Laurie had been "saved" herself, but she was, our speaker confides, always something of a "free spirit," which gives me a tiny feeling of identification with her. Anyway, Wise underwent a great deal of "tribulation," as one might expect, forcing him to pray for God to "enlarge [his] heart and let [him] love the unlovable"—Laurie, that is, who has since been reclaimed by the Lord.

Finally, God took an interest in real estate. There is a long story about a chance encounter that led Wise to a $131-million sale, which was what propelled him to his present wealth. The opportunity appeared in the form of a distinctly unpromising e-mail from a Hotmail address—which elicits a few snickers from the audience, I suppose because it doesn't involve a corporate domain. And even worse, the guy's name was Finkelstein. Wise pauses to let the guffaws die down.

After Larry comes forward to deliver the final blessing, I leap up and gather my stuff. If self-proclaimed Christian busi-

nessmen want to gather for prayer and the exchange of business cards, I have no problem with that. If they want to use
such gatherings as occasions to mock people of different reli-
gions and sexual or political proclivities—well, that is probably within their rights. But when the gatherings are advertised
to job seekers of unknown religion or sexuality—like me, for
example—as gateways to successful employment, the enterprise takes on a sinister cast. Two people approach me for
cards, but I don't stay to chat. All I can think of is escaping
from this place where the ghost of freedom haunts the back-
yards in the form of colorfully dressed, dark-skinned strangers.
Where "Finkelstein" is a laugh line.

THIS WAS NOT my first venture into the extensive territory
where Christianity, so called, overlaps with the business culture. As it happens, that area of overlap has been expanding
rapidly in recent years, to include workplace-based ministries;
employee prayer groups, some at major companies like Coca-
Cola and Intel; networks of Christian businesspeople and
other community leaders; and a growing number of overtly
Christian businesses, some of which identify themselves with a
tiny fish symbol on the product label. According to the *New
York Times,* there were fifty coalitions of workplace ministries
in 1990; today there are thousands.[1] Job seekers are likely to
encounter the Christian business culture at events like the
Norcross Fellowship Lunches—ostensible business meetings
that turn out to be worship services. Or they might be drawn

---

1. Russell Shorto, "Faith at Work," *New York Times Magazine,* October 31,
2004.

to a church-based meeting, advertised as a networking event for the unemployed, that is in fact an occasion for proselytizing. Two months earlier, I had traveled to one of the weekly meetings of the "career ministry" of the McLean Bible Church in northern Virginia, which I had learned about on the web, along with an impressive "success story."

> As long as I believed that jobs were in short supply, that my skills were rusty and therefore not as good as they could be, I wouldn't find a job. So I put together an affirmation, describing the perfect job, the environment I wanted to work in, financial security and the type of people I wanted to work for. I then turned the whole thing over to God. Each day I said this affirmation, thanking God for giving me what I had asked for. I asked that it be made known by the end of July and manifest by September. Within 2 weeks, I received an email with a recruiter's name and phone number from a friend. The rest is a wonderful story of faith and believing. I called this person, went to an open house on July 29 and was hired immediately.

Join us, was the message, and you will soon be on good enough terms with God to give him a firm deadline.

On the evening I attended the McLean Bible Church career ministry, the religious aspects were fairly low-key and devoid of sectarian hostility. The meeting was chaired by Mike, whom I had first mistaken for the pastor. He looked amazed at this error, as if I had gone up to a random Manhattanite on the street and inquired as to whether he or she was the mayor— because the MBC is enormous, almost the size of a small city.

You drive into a parking lot large enough to serve a medium-sized airport, and enter through an atrium that could easily grace an Omni hotel or a very grand bank, where a man at an information booth directs you to your destination in the three-story maze.[2]

Mike opened the meeting by explaining that the "mission of this church is to have an impact on secular D.C. for the Lord Jesus Christ." But it looked as if secular D.C. had already had quite an impact on the church, because I did not, in my wanderings through the building, which includes a "sanctuary" (the basic pew-filled auditorium and pulpit), a cafeteria, a sports area, and much more, see the least item of religious symbolism—no crosses, no Jesus, no angels, nothing. We began with a prayer: "We know you have a plan for our lives . . . Thank you, Father, for being a great provider." An odd reason for gratitude, under the circumstances. During the break, when we were free for informal networking, two of my fellow job seekers, both middle-aged women with computer-related skills, confessed to having had to move back in with their parents after several months of futile searching.

During our half-hour networking time, I had approached a recruiter from Prudential who was cruising the meeting, looking for salespeople, though not, alas, for anyone in PR: "Why aren't you home poring over Monster.com?" I asked, somewhat teasingly, because it had occurred to me that if the job boards really worked, there'd be no need for all this networking. "Well," he said, "you'd be taking a risk to hire someone

2. David Cho, "A Pastor with a Drive to Convert: McLean Sanctuary Opens with Grander Plans," *Washington Post,* June 27, 2004.

from one of the boards; you wouldn't know them." I had persisted, asking him how well he could know someone from a quick face-to-face meeting here. Besides, you're going to interview them anyway, right? But no clear answer was offered.

The pitch, at the MBC career ministry, was delivered by another church volunteer, a thin, tense woman named Lisa, in full business dress. Her profile in the handout we were given reads in part:

> I believe that Jesus is my Lord and Savior. My journey to this place of peace and joy was brought about through trials and tribulation. I found myself at the door of the Career Ministry as a seeker and often wondered what I was seeking for—I came looking for a job and found life! . . . I am a Human Resources professional with 11+ years of experience in the service, retail and hospitality industries.

It didn't look like a place of peace and joy. All through the proceedings, which consisted mostly of going around the room and announcing our names and occupations, I had been thoroughly distracted by Lisa, who stood near the front, although she was hardly the designated center of attention, trying on one facial expression after another—cocking her head to one side with a droll little moue, for example, then suddenly turning back to the paper on which our names and aspirations were being recorded with a studied frown, which could just as quickly give way to a joyless grin. You might have thought she was an alien, sent to Earth with a repertory of facial expressions but no instructions as to when to apply them. She was, I suppose, just looking for the right corporate mask.

At the end of the evening, she bustled to center stage, if

someone so thin can bustle, and essayed a deeply serious look, lips pursed, which was soon replaced by one of embarrassed humility. The idea was that we should buy CDs containing the pastor's sermons on getting through hard times, including his well-known sermon on the war in Iraq. It had helped Lisa pray, and two weeks later she had two job offers. There were no takers, as far as I could see, for the CDs.

Back at the Homestead Suites that night, a stripped-down, generic sort of place near Dulles Airport, I was struck by how much my motel room resembled the church. Not literally, but in the sense of some underlying aesthetic—the same economy of line, neutral colors, cheap indestructible furniture, extremely short-haired carpet for easy cleaning. The room was actually cheerier than the church, thanks to the vaguely impressionist print on the wall. In my exhausted state, it seemed to me that this aesthetic permeates all aspects of the world I have entered: narrative-free résumés dominated by bullets; motel-like, side-of-the-highway churches; calculated smiles; sensuality-suppressing wardrobes; precise instruction sheets; numerous slides.

It works, more or less, this realm of perfect instrumentality; it makes things happen: deadlines are met; reservations are made; orders delivered on time; carpets kept reliably speck-free. But something has also been lost. Weber described the modern condition as one of "disenchantment," meaning "robbed of the gods," or lacking any dimension of strangeness and mystery. As Jackson Lears once put it, premodern people looked up and saw heaven; modern, rational people see only the sky. To which we might add that the minions of today's grimly focused business culture tend not to look up at all. But then what to make of the growing Christianization of business? Will it lead to a kinder, gentler, more reflective business culture? Or is it religion that will have to change, becoming more like the thoroughly utilitarian McLean Bible Church—a realm drained of all transcendence and beauty?

NOTHING HAD COME OF the McLean Bible Church venture— not a single tip for a "seasoned PR professional," willing to relocate anywhere. At the end of the event, I had gone up to our leader, Mike, and asked for his advice. He gave me the name of another church volunteer who would be able to help me, but this guy failed to respond to my calls or e-mails. The Norcross Fellowship Lunch had been equally useless. Still, I can't write off the faith-based approach to job searching on the basis of two bad experiences, and, besides, here in Atlanta, the churches seem to be where the serious networking goes on.

After the Norcross lunch, my next destination is the Crossroads Jobseekers' meeting at the Mt. Paran Church of God, another offering from the Godel web site. Like the McLean Bible Church, this one is a vast multiservice center, but on a slightly smaller scale. No information booth awaits me at the entrance, only a series of dimly lit corridors. I am wandering in search of a human guide when three medium-sized, possibly feral children rush shrieking out of the darkness. No, they have no idea of where the Crossroads meeting might be taking place, and continue on their chase. I walk by rooms labeled for ESL meetings, child care, and support groups for mothers, marveling at all the faith-based social services that are evidently filling in for public and secular ones. Finally, I encounter a black man pushing a broom, who is able to direct me. It's an odd space that I end up at, with a fake house facade at the front, decorated with geranium-filled window boxes, and surrounded by fake potted trees—a permanent stage set, in fact. At the door, a table is laid out with plates of sugar cookies, bottles of soda pop, and a stack of notebooks, which a church volunteer invites me to help myself to.

I'm a few minutes late, due to my wanderings in the church complex, and a woman identified by her name tag as Anna is already speaking from the podium. Other than the church volunteers, only ten people are present, all of whom seem too wrapped up in the presentation to acknowledge my entry, even with a nod. But listening is unnecessary since Anna is going through the notebook we've already been given, on the theme of helpful web sites for job seekers. While she speaks, two monitors on the sides of the stage display the web sites under consideration, so that we are getting the same information from three sources: Anna, the notebook, and the monitors. I concentrate on Anna, noting the carefully put-together earth-toned outfit—could it be that all women of a certain age are assigned to earth tones?

One of the web sites mentioned catches my attention: something called Jobfiler, which organizes your job search for you—your contacts, interviews, et cetera. What I have learned so far is that job searching is almost a profession, or at least a full-time occupation, and now comes the information that this profession, too, is facing technological obsolescence. In my experience, and you may take this as an excuse if you want, anything that promises to "organize" your life is going to take more time than simply continuing to wade through the mess. Still, it's tempting to imagine turning my futile and increasingly messy efforts over to Jobfiler. Or maybe there's some low-wage person in Bangalore who could be paid to do the searching for me.

Digressing from the notebook, Anna counsels us not to despair over a perceived lack of skills, since "the average person has between eight and twelve skills," though she doesn't mention what they may be. In my growing impatience, I want to ask whether eating with chopsticks counts as a skill, but no one is asking anything. My fellow seekers, insofar as I can see their faces without seeming inattentive to the lecture, wear the same dogged, passive expressions I've learned to associate with job seekers everywhere. Maybe the fear is that the slightest sign of impertinence could lead someone in the group to withhold a valuable tip? Anna winds up with an exhortation to always remember what we're worth: "The most important person who ever lived died for you." The image on the monitors changes from that of a perky home page to a deep blue pattern bearing the message "Giving the World Hope in Christ."

My own hope is that we will move on speedily to the networking phase, where I can meet my fellow seekers, announce my aspirations, and perhaps score a contact or two, which is after all the whole point of being here. But Anna declares that it's time for a "testimony." A white-haired man in a turtleneck shirt and jacket launches into a half-hour-long account of his life with the Lord. He had been at IBM for thirty years before moving to a smaller, friskier, dotcom-type company, only to be laid off in 2001. It was a rough time; a lot of his friends didn't even get an interview for a year. Fortunately, the Lord intervened from time to time, prompting him to take a job at Xerox, although at much reduced pay. No matter, he threw himself into it, working twelve hours a day, seven days a week, which was fine until Xerox asked him to take a further pay cut.

The events so far would have led me to conclude that the Lord was not paying close attention, but our speaker remained firm in his faith. He was praying with a friend one day when he got the feeling that the Lord wanted him to take an engineering job that he had applied for. He knew the Lord was with him at this point because when an occasion for sin arose, he was able to just say no, although this was the kind of thing he wouldn't have passed up in his less Christian past. Anyway, he got the engineering job that he still holds. So the kicker is: "Never forget that the Lord can do something that can dramatically change your situation."

At this point it's after eight and I am decidedly hungry. I'm considering an escape when a fellow named François takes over and demands that we all come and sit in a circle around him. This must be the point when the networking will take place, and with so few people present, there should be plenty of opportunity for give-and-take. But no, he launches into what I now recognize as Job Search 101: the need for an elevator speech, a polished résumé, and of course the need to network, network, network. Networking is so central to life, he confides, that we should be taught how to do it in kindergarten and primary school. And who should be our first networking target? The Lord.

I'm sorry, this is too much for me. I endured the Norcross Fellowship Lunch as an atheist, but now, at the Mt. Paran Church of God, I discover I am a believer, and what I believe is this: if the Lord exists, if there is some conscious being whose thought the universe is—some great spinner of galaxies, hurler of meteors, creator and extinguisher of species—if some such being should manifest itself, you do not "network" with it any more than you would light a cigarette on the burning bush. François is guilty of blasphemy. He has demeaned the universe as I know it.

I rise to my feet and gather up my papers, observed with alarm by the three women who are running things: Annie, Judy, and Anna. As I approach the door, Annie scurries over to demand, "Is everything OK? Will you come back?" She walks with me to the stairs and even starts down them with me, clutching at my elbow the whole time. "You should go to the Perimeter Mall Jobseekers' meeting tomorrow morning," she insists; "Why, there are even recruiters who show up there." It's at Fuddruckers, she says, pronouncing that word very slowly, perhaps to forestall any scrambling of the consonants. "It starts at seven thirty, and you can be out of there by ten, when the stores open in the mall."

I LEAVE THE church with every intention of skipping the Perimeter Mall meeting, since my Christian-job-search encounters have led so far only to aversion, though "false pride" is probably the correct theological term. No contacts, no tips, no progress at all on the job-search front. But two things push me to the Perimeter Mall: first, Annie mentioned that I can get there by MARTA, the commuter train system (there's a stop right next to the hotel), and, second, I wake up naturally at the ghastly hour of 4:45 A.M. There is no excuse.

When I enter the restaurant at 7:32, a speaker has already begun. Around forty people sit around at little tables surrounding the makeshift lectern—the usual mostly white, almost all-male group. Since our speaker is a lawyer, he leads off with lawyer jokes: What's the difference between a dead dog on the freeway and a dead lawyer? There are skid marks in front of the dog. A fiftyish man in business casual—this is, after all, Friday—is introduced to give us another "testimony," this one going all the way back to childhood. He attests to having had loving parents, "but there was not much personal relationships or communication" in his natal home. Hence, after sports, college, meeting a nice girl, et cetera, et cetera, his marriage fails, plunging him into depression. He marries again but knows that he hasn't changed.

Now things get vaguer and somewhat more complex. He makes a friend, who is really smart and "takes an interest" in him. They argue a lot, to the point where his wife worries that he might offend the friend. But it is this friend who introduces him to the Bible: "I couldn't argue with the Bible. It just makes sense—good common sense."

I try, and fail, to think of what parts of the Bible can be reasonably accused of making "good common sense." Perhaps our speaker is referring to some alternative Bible that has been purged of miraculous content for easier consumption by the business community, because it is not, as far as I know, the business of religion to "make sense." Now he digresses into the story of Daniel, whom "God took an interest in and got involved in his life." If God could do things for Daniel, our speaker concluded that maybe he could help him too. "The concept that God might be interested in giving me a free gift just dawned on me, and I'm always interested in something free."

Unfortunately for the audience, no striking transformation occurs, no blinding revelation. The narration continues in what appears to be real time—how he prays, argues with his friend some more, always hoping for a freebie from God. Finally, our testifier winds up with the good news that, thanks to his spiritual awakening, he is now "able to have relationships" and remains married to his second wife.

In the testimonies I have heard so far at Christian gatherings, God is always busily micromanaging every career and personal move: advising which jobs to pursue, even causing important e-mails to be sent. In one conversation, a job seeker implied to me that God had intervened to prevent him from selling his house; at least he took the house's failure to sell as "a sign." Thus everything happens "for a reason," even if it is not immediately apparent, and presumably a benevolent one. This vision of a perpetually meddling deity satisfies what Richard Sennett calls the need for a "narrative" to explain one's life. Narratives, he writes,

> are more than simple chronicles of events; they give shape to the forward movement of time, suggesting reasons why things happen, showing their consequences . . . [But] a world marked . . . by short-term flexibility and flux . . . does not offer much, economically or socially, by way of narrative.[3]

What we want from a career narrative is some moral thrust, some meaningful story we can, as Sennett suggests, tell our children. The old narrative was "I worked hard and therefore succeeded" or sometimes "I screwed up and therefore failed." But a life of only intermittently rewarded effort—working hard only to be laid off, and then repeating the process until aging forecloses decent job offers—requires more strenuous forms of explanation. Either you look for the institutional forces shaping your life, or you attribute the unpredictable ups and downs of your career to an infinitely powerful, endlessly detail-oriented God.

3. Sennett, *The Corrosion of Character*, p. 30.

The crowd has doubled in size by this time; maybe the new-comers knew enough to avoid the testimony. Some of the new people are women, even a few women of color—all of them done up in their corporate best, heavy on the red. After a musical flourish supplied by computer, the moderator gives a brief spiel about the need for a relationship with Jesus Christ, and several volunteers rush around from table to table passing out pocket-size versions of the New Testament including psalms and proverbs. We are now to go into our "breakout groups" in various corners of the room, according to whether we are interested in "how clutter can be an obstacle to God's grace," "finding peace and bliss," or "God's way to a successful life." Of course I should go to "clutter," I say laughingly to my tablemates, three extremely glum middle-aged men, but none of them rewards me with a smile.

Clutter turns out to be the most popular breakout group, so I move on to "successful life," led by the Reverend Jack Pilger, where at least I can find a seat. I attempt a networking-type smile at my new tablemate, Pat, but its only effect is to make him get up from the table and dash off. He returns in a minute, though, with a copy of the handout for me, the famous passage from Corinthians on love, with the stirring line: "And if I have prophetic powers, and understand all mysteries and all knowledge, and if I have all faith, so as to remove mountains, but have not love, I am nothing." Maybe it was a successful smile after all.

The Reverend Jack calls one of the job seekers up to read the Corinthians text aloud for us, and invites us to renew our vows at his church this Sunday. I am hoping for more on love, perhaps an elucidation of the mysterious and beautiful part on how you can throw your body into the flames and have it count for nothing if you do not love, but Jack wants to talk about "excellence," which is illustrated by the story of a completely crippled man who was called to the ministry and succeeded brilliantly by creating his own special telephone ministry. Jack isn't much to look at himself—short and pudgy—but the point is that, with the telephone ministry, people don't have to look at this crippled guy, whose deformities are "distracting." If there is a message here for disabled job seekers, it is not an entirely encouraging one.

Meanwhile, a possible networking target arrives. A young Asian-American, identified on his name card as "Tom It," takes the seat next to me, smiles, and extends his hand. We exchange whispered introductions, in which I learn that his surname is Chang and "It" is for IT. While Jack continues on the theme of excellence, Tom busily scribbles in the margins of his handout containing the Corinthians passage. I can see that he's a tidy-minded, IT-type of fellow, since he has drawn a circle enclosing the word *You* and another around *God,* with arrows connecting the circles in both directions. Suddenly, he leans over and stares at the protein bar I am nibbling on: "How many of those can you eat in a day?" he whispers. I point out the calorie content to him, which is 220, and suggest maybe up to ten. "So," he asks, "it's the amount of calories that determines it?"

Now, between the calories and the Corinthians, I am completely confused. But Tom and I exchange cards and agree to share any relevant contacts that should come our way. Now it's almost 9:00 A.M. and time to reassemble in the main space, where I notice Laimon Godel, who has perhaps been here all along, operating the computer that produces the musical flourishes.

We newcomers get to say a few words apiece, just our names and what kinds of jobs we're looking for, so I learn I've been among account managers, systems architects, financial service providers, systems testers, and other people whose daily tasks I can only foggily imagine. The introductions go on and on, with perhaps eighty people in all standing to announce their professions.

In this, the final half hour, a carnival mood sets in. The moderator is presiding over the dispensation of job tips, almost all of which deal with IT, and Laimon is embellishing them with sound effects—trumpet blasts, honking noises, canned laughter—to the apparent delight of the men who are running the meeting from the front of the room. At some point the word *Massachusetts* comes up, as a job location, and elicits a hearty laugh, I suppose because the Massachusetts state legislature has been discussing gay marriage this week. The moderator joins in the laughter, saying, "I've done worse. I used to live on a farm."

General laughter at this—what?—proud assertion of bestiality? I glance over at a somewhat effeminate man at a neighboring table who had caught my attention earlier with his flamboyant—given the setting—outfit of black leather jacket, high white turtleneck, and slim-cut black jeans. He has a thin, strained smile on his face.

After a final blessing I make my way across the room to a familiar face. It's Ken, the quiet guy from Patrick Knowles's boot camp, and he sort of recognizes me too. I tell him I've seen Patrick since the boot camp and that he doesn't seem to be doing too well. "He can be his own worst enemy," Ken responds complacently. "I mean, he's brilliant, but . . ."

How's his search going? Ken says he's got a job and is starting Monday. So why is he here today? To thank some people, say good-bye. I tell him I kind of resent all the religion at this event.

"It's fine with me," he says. "I'm religious myself."

"So where will you be working?" I ask.

"At my old place, where I got laid off a year ago."

"How do you feel about going back there? I mean after they laid you off."

"Oh, no problem." He smiles beatifically. "They didn't need so many people then, and now they do."

So this is the new ideal Christianized, "just in time," white-collar employee—disposable when temporarily unneeded and always willing to return with a smile, no matter what hardships have been endured in the off periods.[4] Maybe one of the functions of the evangelical revival sweeping America is to reconcile people to an increasingly unreliable work world: you take what you can get, and praise the Lord for sending it along.

As we are all milling toward the door, I am approached by an intense-looking man of about forty-five. "You're looking for something in PR?" he asks. I nod eagerly. "You should join the Georgia state branch of the Public Relations Society of America," he advises. "They have a group for PR people in transi-

4. The laid-off IBM employees studied by Sennett tended to withdraw from civic engagement and, at the same time, become more involved in their churches. One of them told Sennett, "When I was born again in Christ, I became more accepting, less striving" (*The Corrosion of Character,* p. 130). In recent self-help literature, Christians are encouraged to see the workplace as a site for "witnessing," proselytizing, and otherwise advancing their religious goals. Kim Hackney's book, *Thank God It's Monday: Celebrating Your Purpose at Work* (Grand Rapids, MI: Baker Books, 2003), for example, is advertised on www.praize.com as offering advice on "living out your God-given purpose at work" and "transform[ing] attitudes about the 'daily grind' and find[ing] satisfaction and joy in your job."

tion." At last, a meaningful tip; maybe enough to redeem this long, strange morning of bowdlerized Christianity leavened with down-home homophobia.

My taxi driver back to the Atlanta airport is an immigrant from India who hopes to become a Pentecostal preacher. When I admit to not being a Christian, he squints back skeptically at me in the rearview mirror, as if he might have missed some telltale facial flaw.

"It's too hard to be a Christian," I explain. "Jesus said that as soon as you get any money, you have to sell all you have and give to the poor."

"Where does it say that?" he asks, genuinely curious.

six

Aiming Higher

Home again, I sit down to confront the fact that my résumé, which has been posted on Monster.com and HotJobs for over two months now, has netted not a single legitimate inquiry. Oh, I get plenty of e-mail, most of it from "executive job search" firms professing to see great promise in my résumé and offering to guide me toward a job in exchange for several thousand dollars. But the health and biomedical companies I have pelted with applications maintain their supercilious silence. I am a fairly compulsive person, at least when it comes to deadlines, and can't help but feel anxious that the one I set for finding a job is bearing down on me with merciless speed.

An ordinary job seeker might despair, but I have a unique advantage: I can simply upgrade my résumé. The key to the upgrade is the knowledge, gained from chatting with other seekers, that many in the PR field are failed journalists—no shame in that, since most newspapers pay shockingly low wages and hardly anyone manages to support him- or herself as a freelancer these days. What this means is that I can draw on more of my actual life as a skeleton for Barbara Alexander's. I cannot cite articles I have written, of course, because someone might ask to see them, but I can truly claim to have taught at the University of California, Berkeley, in the Graduate School of Journalism, where I have a faculty friend willing to confirm, if anyone asks, that Barbara Alexander taught a course called "Writing to Persuade" that was wildly popular with students.

Furthermore, the event planning has to go. I thought that having two "skill sets" would double my attractiveness to employers, but it may have the unfortunate effect of making me look "unfocused." Besides, I've been coming to see event planning as a somewhat sketchy profession, too closely related to catering, and my networking has led to the impression that few companies maintain an in-house event-planning capability anyway. To replace it, I expand on my imaginary PR experience, which now blooms into some full-time jobs, rather than mere consulting. All of these fake jobs are, lamentably, within the nonprofit sector, and although I humiliate myself (my real self that is) by trying to find someone to lie for me within one of the actual for-profit PR firms I've had dealings with over the years, I am stuck with a shady nonprofit past.

Still, it seems to me, the new résumé is impressive. There are no Gaps to cover over with ingenious stories, only a life of solid toil in the service of press relations and image management. I retain my recent history as an independent consultant, but gone is the last trace of Barbara the dabbler and displaced homemaker, replaced by a highly focused, if not workaholic, professional. I post the new résumé on Monster, HotJobs, CareerBuilders, guru.com, workinpr.com, prweek.com, a few job boards in my own state, and the Public Relations Society of America web site—warning myself not to rush to my e-mail the next morning expecting a blizzard of responses. But I must be a glutton for disappointment, because of course that's just what I do.

Next on the agenda is follow-up. I have a stack of business cards from my various trips, and now I e-mail every one of these contacts, inquiring as to how their searches are going, and asking if they have come across any leads for me. Not everyone answers, and no one has a tip. Billy, the guy I had clashed with at Patrick's boot camp over Clinton's homicide record, invites me to the new job seekers' group he has established. Leah, the marketing person I met at the Roasted Garlic, is growing increasingly desperate. Another boot-camp veteran, Richard, the realtor with the permanent wince, surprises me by writing that he has been trying to reach me by phone, because he "just really wanted to talk." He hasn't gotten through because he's been trying my cell phone, which I tend to ignore when I'm at home. Could he take me out to dinner next time I'm in Atlanta? I let his ardor cool for a few days before replying that, yes, dinner would be delightful, but by the time I get back to him he has relocated to Chicago and found a job, the nature of which I cannot elicit, something makeshift, he says, meaning a little bit shameful and hopefully temporary.

MY NEXT, and far more intimidating, follow-up target is Ron of ExecuNet and, before that, the Republican National Committee. I write him a sucky but fairly honest e-mail about how edifying his workshop was and how much I appreciated his

straightforward approach, as opposed to the mushy, semithera-
peutic offerings of your typical career coach, and I remind him
of his promised contact for me. This summons forth a gracious
enough response, ending with a request to refresh his memory
re my situation and skill set. I should send him a résumé, but
which one? I had taken the old one to the ExecuNet session
and don't dare send him the new one, in case he compares it to
the first one and notices how much my experience has ex-
panded in just a few weeks.

So the old résumé goes out to him, along with a renewed reminder about the contact, and when this gets no response, I
write again, asking if he can spare just twenty minutes of his
time for a chat. That was one of his own recommendations:
anyone can be imposed on for twenty minutes of face time. An
e-mail comes back listing several openings in his schedule on
the day I plan to be in Washington, including some noonish
possibilities, so I brazenly offer to take him to lunch, and, im-
probably enough, he accepts.

The obvious site for the rendezvous is the restaurant in the
hotel where I'm staying on Ehrenreich business, which I scout
out at breakfast time and determine to be, if not a reliable food
source, at least a soothingly pseudo-upscale environment. I
prepare meticulously in my room: tan suit, black pullover, gold
earrings. My face gets the full Prescott treatment: foundation,
blush, eyeliner, lip-liner, mascara. I force myself to slow down
and make small, fretful movements with the various pencils
and brushes, since, for some unknown anthropological reason,
bold, broad-stroked face paint has the undesirable effect of
suggesting savagery or sports mania. Examining myself in the
full-length mirror, I conclude that I rock, and that, with the addition of a gold necklace and lapel pin, I might, in Prescott's

judgment, even pass for a Republican. "Clear mind, skillful driver," I recite to myself from Morton's little koan. "Sound spirit, strong horse."

Ron, too, is looking far more "accessible" than he had been—tie-less, with the top button of his button-down pale blue shirt undone. As soon as we are seated, I launch into a summary of my job-search findings, keeping things at the sociological, rather than personal, level, to indicate a lack of desperation. "I get the impression that the whole executive life cycle has changed a lot in the last few decades," I tell him, "and that a lot of people just aren't prepared, emotionally or any other way." Hoping to establish my hereditary membership in the executive class, I cite my father, who worked for Gillette for over twenty years and identified so deeply with the firm that no competing products were allowed in the house. Now, however, people seem to be churned out of their companies every three years or so. Ron confirms my impression; an executive today can count on having eight to nine jobs in a lifetime. "You always think the next job will be the last one, but it never is."

When it comes time to order, I make the mistake of being friendly to the waiter. The correct, Ron-like stance toward the waitstaff, I see, is one of indifference, laced with hostility. He complains, for example, that his water glass is *too full,* and, although it would be no big trick to sip off the offending excess, he has the waiter bring him a new, less generously filled, glass of water. No apology for this shameless fussiness, no "please," not even a moment's eye contact, accompanies the request, leaving me to give the waiter a covert roll of the eyes, a sort of "See what I have to put up with?"

Now to my real problem. I lay out for him one possible strategy, with ample credit to the ExecuNet session for helping me to think "strategically": I will continue to zone in on the pharmaceutical companies but with a letter pointing out their current PR problems—due to high prices and numerous cases of deceptive and fraudulent behavior—and suggest that I can help.

He likes this. "It's good to focus on something like the pharmas. And whoever you're applying to, it's good to refer to the 'pain points' "—meaning what they're doing wrong that you could fix. "But you've got to give them a solution."

"I understand the consumer anger," I say, "but I don't think the pharmas have ever tried to mobilize the goodwill that's out there for them. Among women, for example: You have the birth control pill; you have Tamoxifen. They've changed our lives. They've *saved* our lives." Naturally, I'm leaving out the harm they've done: the high-estrogen birth control pill, hormone replacement therapy, the Dalkon shield, et cetera.

"Good," he says, "so you can suggest a *community* approach."

Ah, that's the word. Now our food arrives, and I am alarmed to see that the chicken piccata comes with a marinara sauce, which is a sufficient danger to the job hunter that Jeffrey J. Fox's book even includes a chapter titled "Don't Order Linguini with Marinara Sauce." One false move with the fork could be death to the tan suit, so I am condemned to tease my appetite with tiny, meticulously executed bites.

"But remember," Ron is telling me, "nothing replaces networking. How are you going to network with the pharmas?" I should, he suggests, start showing up at events and meetings of the PR professional association, mingling, and, in the process, learning where the likely jobs are. Another strategy would be to buy a share of stock in the company I'm interested in and show up at the annual meeting, where anyone can hobnob with the top people "unless you're a troublemaker."

"Mmm." I have to own a bit of a company to work at it? I decide to ask a question that's been on my mind for months: Why, when job searching could be totally rationalized by the Internet through a simple matching of job seekers' skills to company needs, does everything seem to depend on this old-fashioned, face-to-face networking? After all, there's going to be an interview anyway, right?

"It's about trust," Ron answers opaquely, not to mention "likability." "The higher up you get in the executive ranks, the more things depend on being likable. You've got to fit in."

I catch my right hand advancing toward Ron's untouched French fries and quickly revise the gesture into a reach for the salt. It's distracting to think that our major economic enterprises, on which the livelihoods and well-being of millions depend, rest so heavily on the thin goo of "likability."

When we hit the coffee phase, I remind him again of the promised contact. OK, he says, he can give me one "freebie." But now comes the serious pitch: if I would like to be introduced to members of his "support group" of actually employed executives, I will have to pay 4 percent of my last year's salary up front, then 4 percent of whatever salary I land. I realize I can't pretend to earn a low enough figure to make Ron's 4 percent affordable because I had already claimed to be making $100,000 a year in order to qualify for the ExecuNet session, so we're talking at least $4,000. This would buy me endless interview coaching, résumé rewriting, and a chance to eat breakfast every other week with the bigwigs.

He makes it clear that it is something of an honor even to be invited to spend my money in this way; they don't take everybody. "A person with an overblown ego, for example, is not going to do too well in the job-search process." He, Ron, would not have come to lunch with me if he didn't know that "we have the same values." I nod emphatically, not sure what those values could be.

SURE ENOUGH, my freebie arrives by e-mail the next day—a contact at a D.C.-based PR firm called Qorvis.[1] I have applied to only a few PR firms until now, both because I have seen few job openings at them and because I would prefer to be embedded in a corporation with some larger, non-PR mission. I fire off a résumé with a cover letter mentioning Ron in the first line. That done, I begin to draft a new cover letter for pharmaceutical companies, advertising my "community approach" to their unfortunate image problems, which I blame of course on overly zealous regulators and reporters.

There is one last suggestion from Ron to explore: that I become active in the public relations professional society and use it as a means of networking. I had already attempted to follow up on the tip I got at Fuddruckers, and had contacted the Georgia branch of the Public Relations Society of America, but its group for PR folks in transition no longer seemed to be functioning. Ron made a solid case for renewed efforts in this direction: not only do I need to network with actually employed PR people, but it wouldn't hurt to use my "transition time" to expand my PR skills and hence my résumé.

At the PRSA web site, which I repair to almost daily for job

---

1. Qorvis's principal client, I later learn, is Saudi Arabia, which would have represented a considerable ethical stretch even for me.

listings, I comb through upcoming conferences and finally settle on a conveniently timed "professional development seminar" on the theme of "crisis communications management,"
which will include what to do when, for example, "the activists
attack" or the CEO is indicted. It's a huge investment—an
$800 fee plus travel and two nights in a hotel—and it's not for
just anyone off the street. The application form on the web site
demands that I list a current employer, and isn't satisfied until
I finally come up with "Alexander and Associates." Even if it
doesn't pan out as a source of contacts, the session should be,
at the very least, a rare glimpse into the corporate world at its
most vulnerable, and a corporate vulnerability can always be
translated into a potential job. You have activists storming
your headquarters while the CEO is being led off in chains? I
can help, or at least I will now find out how to.

The seminar is held in a hotel in downtown Boston, in yet
another windowless meeting room. Outside, it's a blustery
spring day, lit with occasional flashes of sunshine, and I resent
being condemned to the tomb-like stillness of artificial air and
light. But there's work to be done. I arrive well before nine to
get a head start on the networking, and quickly introduce myself to a half dozen of the thirty or so assembled PR people,
asking them each what sort of crises they face in their industries, outside of the obvious tornadoes and terrorist attacks. I
meet Lori from Coca-Cola, whose concern is product safety,
Roger from Allstate (disgruntled policyholders), two people
from a poultry-processing company (avian flu), and several
people who work for hospitals (unexplained deaths and neighborhood resistance to territorial expansion). Aha: I had
thought of the corporate world as an impenetrable fortress,
but it turns out to be under heavy siege.

At precisely 9:00 A.M. our leader, Jim Lukaszewski, opens the seminar by announcing, "I'll be driving this bus . . . unless someone decides to topple me"—a curious possibility to implant in us, especially given Jim's obvious "likability." He flatters us by declaring us "a group of very senior people" who just need to learn to think "from a different perspective," which is a "management perspective." Forget dealing with the media; our challenge is to "get to the table," where we'll have the attention of management, and then to communicate with them in a language they can understand, "on the spot" and "in real time." Once, things took place over the course of days, but now, thanks to e-mail, et cetera, we are talking minutes. When a crisis breaks out, you have a "golden hour" in which to craft your response and sell it to management.

We start with a video on the cyanide-in-the-Tylenol case, moving from the tragic deaths to their redemption with the introduction of the tamper-proof safety seal. So far so good. I am mightily relieved that there's nothing being said that I can't understand—no mysterious jargon or fake PR science—and nothing being recommended that I couldn't actually do (assuming no ethical hesitancy, that is). Maybe this *is* the right calling for me. I like my fellow seminar participants, none of whom appears to look down on me for being a "consultant" or exhibits the unbearable upbeatness that Kimberly insisted is a prerequisite for employment. Jim even has a sense of humor, or at least a willingness to insert a wicked little "heh heh" here and there in his spiel.

I am eager to get onto the juicy things like antiglobalization activists and CEO indictments, but almost all of the first day and much of the second is devoted to the delicate internal problem of "getting to the table" and attracting the attention of management. This would seem to be pretty far from my own concerns, since I can't even get in the door, and am unlikely to be allowed anywhere near the table without an apron on and a tray in my hand. But I'd at least like a glimpse into the inner sanctum that I may never penetrate in person—behind the glass walls and the checkpoints, in the "C-suites" where the CEOs, CFOs, COOs, et cetera, make their decisions. Jim, who has advised scores of companies during outbreaks of crisis and appears to be a heavy hitter in the PRSA, may be the perfect guide.

The most important thing to understand about management, he tells us, is that they are different from you and me— in particular, they are severely "out of touch." As an example of out-of-touchness, he cites the CEO who asked him (Jim renders this question in a faux snarling voice), "When is this environmental fad going to go away?" And you see, he didn't get it, Jim says in his own voice, because this "environmental fad" isn't going away; it's only getting bigger.

And why is top management so out of touch? Because they are so isolated and, to tell the truth, idle. "All of you have been on the management floors of your company," Jim says. "Notice how quiet it is up there? Because no one is *doing* anything there. Oh, there are a few meetings now and then . . ." We have to understand that the people at the top are lonely people—very lonely. There's only one CEO, so he or she—Jim is scrupulous in his gender inclusiveness even when it's hardly necessary, as in the case of CEOs—has no one to talk to, and everyone around him or her is "waiting to see how far they'll fall." In fact, the average tenure for a CEO is down to a mere thirty months, Jim claims. Thus the CEO is the last to hear the gossip, except in the case he cites of a CEO who was a smoker and had to pursue his habit on the roof of the building along with his nicotine-oriented underlings.

All this casts an entirely new light on the CEO, who tends to be portrayed as an overpaid tyrant, but might be better described as one of the mythical kings in James Frazer's classic book *The Golden Bough*, who is sacrificed in the spring to fructify the soil. Or the Aztec sacrificial victims who are fattened and coddled for weeks before the ceremonial excision of their hearts.

Before I can get carried away with sympathy for these doomed and lonely men, though, Jim is outlining how they spend their time: less than 5 percent on decision making, 40 percent on "articulating" those decisions, 40 percent on "teaching, motivating, and coaching," 20 percent on "repeating and explaining," 5 percent on "admiration building" (that is, "looking for compliments"), and 1 percent on "reputation building" (it's not clear whether this is the reputation of the company or of the CEO himself). No, it doesn't add up to 100 percent, but that's because CEOs are responsible "24/7." Jim immediately contradicts this, however, by observing that, any time you really need them, like in a crisis, top management is in Bimini or Barbados.

At this point Jim is beginning to sound like an antiglobalization activist himself: he's on the environmentalists' side; he's portrayed CEOs as vain, curmudgeonly fellows who spend large chunks of their time basking in Barbados or swanning around looking for compliments. But guess what? We owe them our total loyalty. Our goal in fact is to become their trusted advisers—*consiglieri* is the word that comes to mind. Sometimes we (PR people) get confused and think we're working for the media. "How many of you have been journalists?"

he asks, and about a fourth of the people in the room raise their hands. Well, forget all that. "Reporters are fundamentally unhappy people." As PR people, we don't even have to return their phone calls, he tells us—to a visible shiver of discomfort in the room. Concentrate on solving the crisis, or getting management to solve the crisis, and ignore the media till you're ready to talk to them.

It's the internal culture of the corporation, as seen by Jim, that fascinates me. The picture he paints resembles one of the royal courts of Europe, circa 1600, as described by Castiglione or, closer to our own time, the historian Norbert Elias. We, the PR people, are the courtiers who both despise the king and eagerly press around him, anxious for a moment of royal attention. We must learn to speak in low, quiet tones, always framing our advice "strategically" and never wasting words on anything he already knows. Only if we can insinuate ourselves into his confidence can we hope to save the country—I mean, the company—and of course all the credit will go to him.

At our group lunch I learn that some of my fellow participants are getting impatient with the endless lecture on dealing with management. They expected something more participatory and hands-on, with a chance to workshop their way through various mock crises. It is odd, in fact, that while Jim stresses the need for brevity in communications with management, he has no such constraint in dealing with us. After all, most of what he's been telling us is already in the notebook he's passed out to us, available for reading at our leisure. Maybe, after so many struggles to get to the table, he's just reveling in this opportunity to get up on it and dance for hours on end.

I firm up my networking with Lori, learning that Coke endured a major management shake-up for failing to deal promptly with a bacterial-tainting issue in Europe. I have a long talk with the woman who handles PR for the National Forest Service in Montana, that being my home state, about the relative merits of Livingston and Missoula. I chat with Alexandra, who is wearing blue jeans and works for a California company that arranges overseas outsourcing for American firms. "Why should people be angry at you, when these firms are going to outsource anyway?" I ask. "That's what I'm always saying," she tells me, looking harried by invisible pursuers.

I approach Roger from State Farm and ask him to outline for me, as a newcomer to the corporate world, his "typical day." When it turns out to involve ten hours at his desk, I ask whether the demands decrease as he rises in the hierarchy. For a moment his smile fades; no, with each accomplishment, the expectations only increase. Everyone graciously accepts my card and promises to contact me should any job come to their attention.

In the afternoon session I have plenty of time to ponder the paradox of Jim, searching for clues as to what is expected of a serious PR professional. He is nice, no doubt about it, even liberal in certain ways. When the subject of unions briefly comes up, and he remarks that they're "dying," someone in the group interjects "not fast enough!"—leading Jim to defend the working class. We need to "look at unions with understanding." "Businesses own everything," he continues in a Marxist vein. "All the workers own is their contract." His own father was a blue-collar union member, and "if you want to see democracy in action, go to a union meeting." At one point, he reveals that four people on the staff of his own PR firm are currently involved—in their private lives, that is—on the community side of various struggles. "Activism is fun," he confides, "especially when you spend all day being a corporate apologist. Heh heh."

But in our professional lives, we are the antiactivists and can never forget it. He gives us the case of a real crisis he successfully managed: A hospital in Philly wanted the city's permission to place a helipad on its roof. This was, Jim lets us know, completely unnecessary, since there were already four helipads on hospital roofs within a one-mile radius, but a helipad is a "prestige thing" for a hospital. So what did Jim do to counter community opposition to the helipad? He organized a door-to-door pro-helipad campaign. The campaign was successful; the hospital got its helipad and no doubt the opportunity to treat the stress-related disorders occasioned by the heightened noise level.

Then there is the hypothetical case of community hostility to a big-box store—Wal-Mart comes to mind—in which we are invited to come up with all the good these entities do: create jobs, give consumers choices, pay taxes, et cetera. After these benefits have been listed on the flip chart, he surprises us by announcing that "they're not worth mentioning," because everyone knows they're not true. "So how *do* you promote the big-box store in the community?" I raise my hand to ask. Jim says, "We'll get to that," but we never do. The point, he says, is we have to start by making management aware of how hollow the company's promises sound. Then, presumably, we can launch our own pro-big-box community-organizing drive.

At some point in the middle of the second afternoon, I begin to fantasize about hijacking this "bus," but for purely physical reasons. I have been sitting for more than a day now, not counting the day of air travel getting here, and have just about exhausted my capacity for immobility. The disks in my spinal column are fusing into knots of pure pain; deep vein thrombosis has set into the lower legs; muscles all over my body are liquefying from disuse. Everyone else seems content to be paralyzed, although there are ever more frequent trips to the bathroom or for cell phone use in the corridor, and the Coke gal has been covertly answering e-mail on her BlackBerry. It occurs to me that much of my job search so far has involved sitting in windowless rooms while someone—most commonly a white male in his fifties or sixties—stands at the front testifying, preaching, exhorting, or coaching. Maybe it isn't the content of the presentation that matters, but the discipline required to maintain the sitting posture and vague look of attentiveness for hours on end. While blue-collar workers invite injury and exhaustion through physical exertion, white-collar workers endure the sometimes equally painful results of immobility. Maybe the whole point of a college education, which is the almost universal requirement for white-collar employment, is that it trains you to sit still and keep your eyes open. At the moment, I'd rather be waitressing.

The last thing I remember before falling into a narcotized trance that may have been actual sleep is a long personal digression into the history of the seated posture. When did chairs come into common use? Certainly no more than a few thousand years ago, well after our muscular-skeletal structure achieved its modern form. We are designed for running and walking, squatting and lounging, not for sitting upright day after day.

I don't think I actually pitch forward in my seat or otherwise betray my attention deficit, but there is a moment at least of absolute discontinuity, from which I awake to a slight shuffling in

the room. We have finally gotten to what we've all been waiting
for: the chance to do some problem-solving ourselves. Each of
us is handed a number, from one to five, assigning us to a new
table, and each table will undertake a different "crisis."

Lurid as they are, Jim insists that each one is based on a real
situation: A company runs a free Christmas gift program for
needy children, and one of the wrapped presents turns out to
be a porn tape, provoking much righteous indignation in the
community, especially the churches. A corporate jet crashes
into a neighborhood containing a day-care center. A company
doing community clean-up work in south-central L.A. gets
caught in a shoot-out between the Crips and the Bloods. A
company finds that its baby products cause rashes. I'm in the
group whose company faces a wave of sexual harassment
charges that has attracted the unwelcome attention of a national women's organization (the activists).

Here we are at last, sitting face-to-face instead of all facing
Jim, free to interact, and within minutes I am seriously annoyed. My tablemates, among whom middle-aged males from
the insurance industry are heavily represented, seem to be
uniquely clueless. Someone proposes that we (the company)
provide medical care and counseling for the victims, leaving
me to explain the difference between sexual harassment and
rape, and how an offer of psychiatric counseling to a victim of
sexual harassment might easily be construed as an insult.

But mostly I'm irritated by their flounderingly unsystematic
approach. Jim gave us a general outline to follow, beginning
with establishing a timeline of events, but no one seems to
have been paying attention. Without thinking, I find myself
morphing into ENTJ mode, pounding the table and insisting
on a thorough investigation: "We've got to get the timeline

down. We've got to know why these allegations got to the press before they got to us!"

Someone writes *timeline* on our flip chart, where it joins a series of disconnected entries like *meet with victims* and *sensitivity training,* then we move on to the issue of what to do about the national women's organization that has arrived on the scene. One of the guys at the table suggests that we offer the group a sizable donation to go away. Fools! I picture the redoubtable Kim Gandy, current president of the National Organization for Women, responding to a proffered bribe.

"It doesn't work that way," I interject forcefully. "We're talking about people with *principles.*" Then I proceed to outline how we might go about co-opting the national women's organization more cleverly: Set up an independent commission to investigate the allegations, or pretty independent anyway, and put representatives from the women's organization on it. They'll feel like they're doing something, and it'll make the company look like the best thing that's happened to feminism since *Roe v. Wade.*

Blinking slightly, my tablemates accept this plan. But what am I doing? I'm not here to save Mitsubishi, which went through a major sexual harassment scandal in the nineties and is, I suspect, the prototype for our particular crisis. I'm here to network, which means being likable, as opposed to being successful or right. Everyone else at the table seems happy enough to get along by going along. Abashed, I pull back and content myself with nodding encouragingly as my tablemates continue to spatter their uninspired, nonstrategic entries on the flip chart. Without me, I can see, *they have no plan.* So yeah, I can do this PR thing, without any further training than what life has already afforded me. But only if I'm in charge.

As soon as I get home from Boston I rush to update my résumé on the job boards, adding the impressive-sounding PRSA Crisis Communications Seminar, and start to rethink my cover letters and general approach. What I've learned from Jim is that corporations are scared, if not actually paranoid, and for good reason. Give me an industry, and I can think of a "crisis" menacing it: an angel-of-death nurse in a hospital; a whistle-blower in a chemical company; dissatisfied or injured customers—"that is, *victims,* heh, heh," as Jim had put it in his presentation—anywhere. Thus every company needs a crisis communications plan, whether it knows this or not, as well as a person—that is, me—to design it. In my new cover letters—which go out to all the pharmas I have applied to so far—I explain that the function of PR "is not only to light fires, but to put fires out." If I can sell the threats—the homicides, the lawsuits, the face-painted, anarchistic, antiglobalization activists—I can sell myself as the knight on the white horse, savior of corporations.

And I'm sure now that I can do it. My entire life experience is part of the skill set I will bring to the firm that eventually hires me. Jim makes the perfect role model: Naturally he's a nice guy—that's just part of the job. He's spent hours explaining how challenged corporate management is in the area of values and compassion; so of course it's his job, as a PR person, to compensate. I have some of the same advantages: compassion, empathy, a familiarity with unions and community groups, some notion of the principle-driven life. I can carry all this to the throne, just as Jim has, and set it at the feet of the king.

BUT THE FACT is that no takers are presenting themselves. My one big lead, given to me by Ron in exchange for a $35 lunch, collapses ignominiously. My letter to Qorvis, which asked for no more than a twenty-minute "informational interview" in which to learn about their business, received an encouraging response. But by the time of my follow-up call, the Qorvis guy has gone cold.

"Am I to understand that you've been operating for the past three years as a one-person consultancy?" he asks.

"Well, yes," I tell him, and mindful of Ron's advice that a beggar has to have a good story, go on to burble about how "I've taken an unusually entrepreneurial approach, I admit, and done extremely well with it, but now I'm looking for the camaraderie and shared mission of a firm blah blah."

"Ah" is all he says.

He gives me the names of two others on the "hiring team," whom I diligently pursue with e-mails and phone messages, to no response at all. A consultancy, no matter how energetic and profitable, must count as a Gap. Meanwhile, in addition to maintaining my résumé on the job boards, I am of course applying for every job that shows up on the Public Relations Society of America web site or that comes to me through the Atlanta Job Search Network, and one of the latter suddenly shows a flicker of promise. Locum Tenens, a small company that serves as a temp agency for physicians in the central Georgia area, is looking for a PR director, so I write back emphasizing my extensive involvement in the health-related field and my veritable passion for working with physicians. When I make my follow-up call, Deborah—the designated hiring agent—picks up the phone herself and asks whether I have any questions. Indeed I do, since this encounter will be a test of my expanding skills.

"Do you have any philanthropic involvement in the

community?"—the idea here being that a company's philanthropic activities should be seen, somewhat coldheartedly, as an extension of its PR efforts, and even small companies, to my certain knowledge, can afford to buy a couple of tickets to the annual YWCA or Big Brother, Big Sister luncheon.

Deborah says she's not sure, and seems uncertain as to what "philanthropic involvement" might involve, so I press on, armed by my training with Jim: "Do you have a crisis communications plan? For example, if there were to be complaints about one of your physicians? You know, sexual harassment or an unusual number of deaths."

Again, she's not sure, and while I attempt to alarm her with the absolute necessity of a crisis communication plan, which I am uniquely prepared to create and implement, she must be fishing for my résumé, because she says, "Oh, here you are," and then, after a pause, the familiar rejection: "There's a Gap."

I'm not sure whether she has my original, Gap-ridden résumé, or, like Qorvis, is interpreting the consultancy in the new one as a Gap, and there's no way to check my records while we're on the phone. One thing I've learned, though: a Gap of any kind, for any purpose—child raising, caring for an elderly parent, recovering from an illness, or even consulting—is unforgivable. If you haven't spent every moment of your life making money for somebody else, you can forget about getting a job.

The brief encounter with Qorvis, the nibble from Locum Tenens—these are the exceptions in what is becoming a life of unrelenting rejection. I have, by this time, applied for over 200 advertised and posted jobs, even branching out from health and pharmaceuticals to banks and the trade association for the modular construction industry, which latter at least yields a pleasant phone conversation about the unfortunate down-market image of modular buildings and how this might be corrected by creative PR.

But it is the rare application that generates human contact of any kind. When I can follow up with a phone call, which is not always possible, since named contacts are seldom given, I might be told, as I was by a firm called IR Technologies, that my résumé had entered some complicated industrial batch process, along with hundreds of others, which process could take weeks to resolve. Or I might get a recording saying that "due to the volume of applications, we are unable to verify the status of your application." G.J. Meyer, in *Executive Blues,* reports from his job search in the late eighties that

> unless you're luckier than most or the job market gets a lot better than it has been lately, you'll discover that it's possible to send off five hundred resumes with five hundred customized cover letters and not get a single reply more substantial than a preprinted postcard saying thanks.[2]

That was in a more genteel era. I have received, for all my efforts, only one such preprinted postcard. Usually an automatic response appears in my in-box seconds after electronically submitting my résumé and cover letter, but it offers no thanks, just an acknowledgment of receipt and a code number to use should I be pesky enough to follow up. Mostly there is nothing at all, and it is this—the unshakable, godlike, magisterial indifference of the corporate world—that drives my fellow job seekers to despair. Neal, whom I met at the ExecuNet meeting, told me:

2. Meyer, *Executive Blues,* p. 34.

You ring people and no one returns your calls, or apply by computer and just get an automatic response. I had got to the stage where I'd just get up and sit around and drink coffee until it's time for lunch, really do nothing all day. Dealing with the rejection is quite difficult.

But rejection puts too kind a face on it, because there is hardly ever any evidence that you *have* been rejected—that is, duly considered and found wanting. As the *New York Times* reported in June 2004: "The most common rejection letter nowadays seems to be silence. Job hunting is like dating, only worse, as you sit by the phone for the suitor who never calls."[3] The feeling is one of complete invisibility and futility: you pound on the door, you yell and scream, but the door remains sealed shut in your face. I remember once reading a complaint about the invisibility of middle-aged women in our society, and thinking, *bring it on.* Because invisibility is something every child aspires to—the chance to flit around snatching cookies and making gargoyle faces, immune from punishment. But now, like all those fairy-tale characters who are unfortunate to get what they wished for from an overly literal-minded wish granter, I am left frantically trying to undo the spell. Is it my résumé that consigns me to darkness or, in the case of the people whom I encounter at networking events, something about my physical appearance?

I start fantasizing about ways to bring myself to the attention of the faceless executives, the "hiring managers" on whom the outcome of my search depends. I should develop a new circle

3. Lisa Belkin, "No Yes; No No; No Answer at All," *New York Times*, June 6, 2004.

of friends, more usefully connected than the existing ones. I should get out to parties, like the glitzy one I read about in the *Washington Post* where the CEO of Qorvis was sighted chatting up the political *machers*. Steve, a marketing man and fellow member of the Atlanta Job Search Network, is taking a similarly creative approach to hobnobbing with the decision makers.

> I'm interested in a waitstaff job in the Capitol Grill [an upscale restaurant in downtown Atlanta] . . . where serving gives you a chance to network with the big shots by giving them your business card with the check. The most expensive bottle of wine on the menu costs eight hundred dollars. So I'm going to take a three-day course on wines.

This could be me in a few weeks or months—a cocktail waitress or member of the catering staff, deftly slipping résumés to my customers.

seven

In Which I Am Offered a "Job"

In late May, six months into my search, I get an e-mail request for an actual interview. AFLAC, the insurance company, is looking for sales reps in the central Virginia area, with opportunities for management positions, and my résumé—which they must have come across on one of the job boards—suggests that I may be just the woman for the job. This is not, of course, the first job offer that has found its way to my in-box. There was the one from a verbally disabled firm looking for female models, for example, stating:

> Whats good fam its your boi JR . . . Check us out you wont be sorry. Plenty of pics and video, and guess what? We need new talent so you ladies in Washington DC, Baltimore, Virginia, Atlanta, Ga. and Houston, Texas that are interested in joining our team and ready to make some real money send me a short email along with a photo or two.

I have also been solicited to sell insurance against identity theft, and spent twenty-five minutes on the phone listening to a recorded "conference call" in which two male voices concurred happily that the problem is "growing exponentially." I got a bite from Melaleuca, a United Kingdom–based firm specializing in eco-friendly cleaning products and cosmetics and now seeking sales reps in the United States. In a phone conversation, Melaleuca's Steve assured me that "it's not one of those multilayer marketing-type jobs where you have to put a lot of money up front. It's really a matter of spreading the word in your social life."

"I get paid just to spread the word?" I asked.

"That's right; there's no pressure to perform. It's a word-of-mouth-type business."

I briefly try to envision a social life in which the subject of cleaning fluids would naturally arise on a regular basis, but the money aspect is less than appealing. Steve says he puts twenty hours a week into selling Melaleuca products and grosses about $300 in U.S. dollars, but he has to spend $75 to $80 a month for the products he sells—for a net wage, I calculate, of around $11 an hour.

AFLAC, however, is a highly reputable and successful organization, as far as I know. Everyone has seen its irritating commercials, in which two people are complaining about their insurance problems while, completely unnoticed by them, a duck keeps proclaiming the solution: *AFLAC.* In preparation for my interview, I visit the AFLAC web site, where I learn that the product is "supplemental insurance" to round out the no-doubt inadequate health insurance your employer provides. Then I turn to Google and Nexis, where I hit pay dirt after less than thirty minutes: AFLAC has had problems with the training and management of its sales force. I will stun my interviewer with this information, followed by the unique management contribution I am prepared to make. Furthermore, there are suggestions that AFLAC has overplayed the duck. It's fine for attracting initial attention, but you need a more mature and serious approach if you're selling insurance. That's me—serious and mature—the antiduck.

It's a gorgeous drive over the Blue Ridge Mountains to Staunton, where the AFLAC office is located, but my perilous speed of fifteen miles per hour over the speed limit allows for no scenic appreciation. At the last minute before leaving home, I discovered a dim, archipelago-shaped stain on one sleeve of the tan suit, which required a quickie home dry-cleaning session, but I manage to arrive only five minutes late. The office occupies a far more humble rural site than I expected: half of a one-story building across from a rundown shopping center. Only one car is parked outside, and its vanity plate reads "AFLAC."

Despite my tardiness, Larry greets me enthusiastically and ushers me into a windowless room containing a table and a half-dozen chairs. To enhance the entombment effect, he shuts the door behind us, although, oddly enough, there is not a soul around to disturb us. Where is the bustling, high-energy team promised by the AFLAC web site, the "fun" atmosphere and instant camaraderie? Larry is about fifty, with pale blond hair, wearing a white shirt embossed with the word *AFLAC* and a yellow tie featuring many small ducks. Maybe it would be unwise to bring up the company's alleged overreliance on its barnyard spokesperson, since the only decoration the office contains, in addition to a large photo of the post-9/11 Manhattan skyline, is a rubber ducky on what appears to be a receptionist's desk.

What ensues is not what I would call an interview. Larry offers me a blue folder containing colored sheets of paper starting with one titled "A Career Opportunity with AFLAC" and starts reading aloud from his own folder while I attempt to follow along in mine. This seems to be the preferred method of corporate communication: reading aloud, either from paper or a PowerPoint, while the person being read to reads along too. Is there some fear that no one will pay attention unless at least two senses—auditory and visual—are engaged simultaneously? Occasionally, Larry departs from the script, to tell me, for example, that although AFLAC is "huge," that is not something they dwell on anymore: "You know, after Enron and WorldCom, we don't emphasize the bigness. We're a family-run operation."

Now to the serious part, beginning with a sheet titled "Immediate Income/Paid for Past Efforts/Lifestyle." On the matter of lifestyle, "I don't try to turn people into perfect AFLAC robots," he assures me, though the tie, the shirt, and the vanity plate would seem to suggest that the botlike approach can't hurt. There is a reason for this unusual level of tolerance, he explains: "If we were all the same, how could we open up new markets?" Also, I can work as hard or as little as I want; it's up to me how much I want to "produce." Low production, however, could lead to his flooding my market area with fresh, competing salespeople, and with this he gives me a narrow look. I will want to hit the ground running, he warns, because the first few months' sales count for a lot.

I remind him that, as I wrote in an e-mail, I am not interested in a sales job; I want to *manage* salespeople—motivate them, mentor them, and work with them to devise a strategic approach to our allotted terrain. This, I decide, is the moment for my bombshell: the articles in the business literature arguing that AFLAC has had problems managing its sales force. But if Larry is impressed by my knowledge, he does a good job of concealing it, continuing on unfazed like a tour guide who's been through this museum a few too many times. Yes, yes, I can be a manager, though this seems to require recruiting my own salespeople to manage, just as he is apparently doing right now. There are in fact about ten blue folders spread out neatly on the table, attesting to a strenuous series of "interviews," of which mine could be, for all I know, the eleventh of the day.

On to the money part and a blinding sheet of numbers titled "Income Illustration" and showing that even a complete slacker can make $32,000 in her first year through a combination of commissions, bonuses, and policy renewals. Also, Larry ad-libs, "we have fun"—at company-sponsored trips to destinations like Las Vegas, Honolulu, and San Diego. As he returns to the numbers, highlighting here and there in brilliant yellow-green, I ponder my role in this "interview." Looking interested would seem to be the main thing, and I try on various faces meant to convey agreement, concern, fascination. I must look as freakish as Lisa—the volunteer with the ever-changing expressions at the McLean Bible Church—just sitting here trying on masks.

Business can only get better, he's telling me. Why? Because health insurance deductibles and co-pays are rising steadily, and because "people have less disposable income than at any other time," meaning they can't handle those deductibles and co-pays themselves. I nod cheerily at the good news. Here we are, in a weird corporate niche created by the total failure of the American health-care system, and I am grinning with delight at the deepening misery.

There occurs now the kind of physiological breakdown that could sink a genuine interview. A headache starts pinching in from my right temple; my throat begins to itch. When I break into an uncontrollable fit of alternating coughing and sneezing, he eventually notices and allows me to get some water from the cooler just outside the room. Either I'm allergic to something in the conference room, or carbon monoxide is being pumped in through the vents. Fortunately, we have reached the end of the sheets in the folder, and he asks whether I have any questions.

Yes, I do, like what are we doing in this windowless room while the Blue Ridge Mountains undulate beckoningly outside? But instead I ask him something guaranteed to please: Has he made any inroads into the University of Virginia, which is Charlottesville's largest employer? No, he says, and looks at me for the first time with something approaching interest. Good, I tell him. I have lots of contacts there.

The next step? Some of the people he is interviewing this week will be invited back for a second interview—"that's where we get to know each other." He will let me know next week if I've made the cut. I tell him I'll be away next week but will try to check my e-mail, at which point he says, "Well, why don't we just make an appointment for the second interview right now?" So, just like that, I've made the cut.

DESPITE THE PROMISE that this second interview, which occurs two weeks later, will be our chance to "get to know each other," it proceeds exactly like the first one. Larry, again wearing an AFLAC shirt and duck tie, leads me through the still entirely unoccupied outer rooms to the windowless conference room, where the table is again stacked with blue folders. "I have a present for you," I tell him—a new hardcover book about the advertising agency that created the spokes-duck, sent to me by a friend in the publishing industry whom I had told about my possible AFLAC job. I have read the crucial duck section, in which a young ad man wanders the streets of Manhattan, muttering "AFLAC, AFLAC" over and over to himself, until, in a stunning epiphany, he realizes he sounds like a . . . But Larry is too baffled by this departure from the script to thank me. He glances at the cover, then pushes the book aside with one finger, as if rejecting a bribe.

Out of one of the blue folders (and this is a more advanced set than last time), he takes a bunch of stapled pages titled "Fast Track to Management" and begins highlighting phrases as he speaks them. I can become a CIT (Coordinator in Training) if I produce "a minimum of $50,000 AP" in six months, open a minimum of six new accounts, and recruit at least one other salesperson. Continuing with the "six" theme, I will have six responsibilities as a CIT, including "attending quarterly CDIs with the DSC, RSC, and SSC." I must in addition acquire an insurance broker's license and become "Flex and SmartApp Certified." Any questions?

Now he produces a Xeroxed calendar for July and begins highlighting the days I will spend in training classes, some of which will be conducted in another Virginia city, where AFLAC will pay for my motel room, assuming I am willing to share a room. A laptop will be required.

"Will the company give me one?" I inquire.

"No, but you'll make the money to pay for it in no time at all."

So, not counting the laptop, that's an initial investment of about $1,900 for the broker's license and courses leading up to it. We move on through the content of the courses AFLAC will be offering me, including "L.E.A.S.E. Secretary and Approach Memorization (DSC 1-on-1 Reinforcement)," and "Account Servicing, Billing Reconciliation, and NOI Networking." There will also be training in cold-calling, Larry adds, though this is not written down anywhere, perhaps because a cold call is the salesperson's equivalent of a cold douche; most people would do almost anything to avoid having to make one. I note that the calendar, in which almost every weekday is now high-lighted, indicates both full and new moons, and cannot help but wonder what use an AFLAC associate might make of this information.

He has taken on an increasingly bosslike tone, which I struggle to interpret positively. In the first interview, he was selling the job; now he's directing it. There is the need to clear my calendar immediately, the need to get cracking on the bro-ker's exam, which will require mastery of a huge book. (Larry shows the book to me, though I will have to buy my own, and even he admits it's "boring.") "I hope you realize you've got the job if you want it," he says out of the blue, with nothing more than a quick upward glance from the folder in front of him.

He should smile at this point. He should shake my hand and offer a hearty "welcome to the team." But Larry seems to be too emotionally defended to pause for celebration. In fact, he follows up with an implied put-down. Waving dismissively at a printout of my résumé, he says, "It's not about this. I don't even understand what this is about"—as if my career had been in astrophysics. "I make my judgment based on how a person communicates. Whether they have people skills. Whether they're a good listener." Then he gives me a little nod, for indeed I have been a good listener, though this would seem to be a pretty minimal requirement for an interviewee. He returns seamlessly to the need to "hit the ground running" and "make a total commitment." Any questions?

"What about health insurance?"

"We're independent contractors; we get our own."

So he has people selling health insurance who have none of their own? More tactfully, I ask whether I will have an office to work out of.

"Umm, our associates use their home offices."

We shake hands and I set out to drive home, but some kind of monsoon strikes the mountains, forcing me off the road to sit and stare through the windshield wipers at the whiteout beyond. I have a job. I have been found fit to represent a major corporation to the general public, apparently on no other basis than my ability to sit still and listen meekly for two long and dreary hours. Or maybe I should give myself more credit for appearance and simulated enthusiasm; it's hard to say. That, anyway, is the bright side. On the dimmer side, this "job" offers no salary, no benefits, not even an office with fax machine and phones. I might as well have applied at Wal-Mart and been given a pushcart full of housewares to hawk on the streets. I never call back, nor does Larry call me.

THERE ARE THOUSANDS—tens of thousands—of "jobs" like this available to corporate rejects and malcontents. In 1995, 31 percent of the American workforce found themselves in some sort of "nonstandard" employment, characterized by a lack of benefits and weak bonds to their ostensible employers, and the number continues to grow.[1] Many of these people are pink-collar temp workers and blue-collar day laborers—lawn workers and housecleaners, for example.

But a growing number of the nonstandardly employed are former corporate employees, professionals and managers who have burned out or been expelled from their jobs. For the white-collar job seeker, the lures—or, as the case may be, snares—are everywhere. My in-box always contains one or two exhortations to "Be Your Own Boss!" and "Make as Much Money as You Want!" often accompanied by an eye-catching question like: "Sick of the Corporate Rat Race?" "Got a Case of the MONDAYS?" "Head Hurt From Hitting a Glass Ceiling?" "Lost That Loving Feeling for Your Job?" Recruiters to these quasi employments lurk at networking events, like the fellow I met at Fuddruckers who offered to match me to an appropriate franchising opportunity. I could have my own Merry Maids business, he assured me, and run it by remote control from the location of my choice.

Selling real estate is one of the more respectable and traditional alternatives to the corporate world and offers no more of an initial hurdle than selling insurance: all you have to do is pay for a course and pass a state-licensing exam. My brother does it in Missouri, my brother-in-law in Colorado, as do a number of geographically scattered friends and acquaintances.

---

1. Arne L. Kallenberg, Barbara F. Reskin, and Ken Hudson, "Bad Jobs in America; Standard and Nonstandard Employment Relations and Job Quality in the United States," *American Sociological Review*, 65: 1 (2000), pp. 256–78. In personal communications, Kallenberg and Hudson assured me that the trend is continuing.

My brother is a corporate dropout and former owner of a motel in Arkansas; my brother-in-law came to real estate after a move to escape the high living costs in Hawaii derailed his career as a schoolteacher. When his teaching credentials proved nontransferable to Colorado without a several-thousand-dollar investment in further courses, he managed a Burger King for five years and spent a brief interlude as a paralegal before settling on real estate. One of my Atlanta contacts, a woman with a background in web-site design, has taken the real estate course and is considering taking the state exam. Clark Nickerson, whom I also met at Fuddruckers, had been an industrial sales manager for twenty-seven years and decided to enter the field after an "early retirement" proved financially nonfeasible and a yearlong job search bottomed out.

> By mid-April [2003] I was doing everything you should do—going to networking meetings, using the job boards—but I was really having a hard time staying motivated. My wife and I sat down—she struggles when I do—and she said, "This is just not working." What I realized then was I didn't want to get back into the industrial sales world. She said, "What about real estate?"

But as a default career for the white-collar unemployed, real estate is far from reliable. According to the respected industry magazine *Realty Times*, first-year realtors suffer an 86 percent failure rate, and of those who survive, 70 percent earn less than $30,000 a year. In my brother-in-law's opinion, real estate "is too easy to get into. A lot of people don't really see it as a profession, just an interim thing." For an "interim thing," though, he says the payoffs are slow to come.

You need at least enough money to carry you for a year. I started with four hundred cold calls a week—door-to-door and phone calls—and didn't really make anything for six to eight months. Then, when you get a commission check, you don't realize at first that forty to fifty percent has to come out of it for expenses—everything from taxes to the desk fee a lot of agencies charge. After my first year, I had to get a bank loan just to pay our taxes.

Both my brother-in-law and his wife, my sister, toil away at his real estate business, grossing about $75,000 in 2004, of which half went for taxes and expenses.

In his midfifties and still in the early, nonremunerative phase of his real estate career, Clark Nickerson is hopeful: "It's going good, going great . . . It's a lot of training and learning and basic grunt work, but I'm fully confident that I'll have some clients and listings soon." All I could think of, when Clark told me this, was Cynthia, the woman who burst into tears at Patrick's boot camp, and Richard, who appeared to be on the verge of doing so himself—two realtors who had been unable to stay afloat and were restarting their job searches from scratch.

Another nonstandard form of employment held out to the unemployed is franchising, known to cynics as "buying yourself a job" because the initial fee for the right to use the corporate franchisor's name is in the $15,000 to $40,000 range.[2] In an earlier era, people were more likely to start their own small businesses; today you can buy a sort of prefab business, in which operating procedures, as well as any products used or

2. According to www.francorp.com. Francorp bills itself as "The Leader in Franchise Development and Consulting."

sold, are supplied, for a monthly "royalty," by the franchisor. About 400,000 Americans are franchisees, managing eight million employees and generating one-third of U.S. gross domestic product—everything from doughnuts and burgers to fitness centers. But as in real estate, the rewards are uncertain and the prospects of failure dauntingly high. In his study of franchisees in a variety of industries sociologist Peter M. Birkeland found a survival rate of only about 25 percent and average franchisee incomes of about $30,000.[3]

Finally, as an option for the white-collar unemployed, there are thousands of commission-only sales jobs such as the one AFLAC offered me. According to the Direct Selling Association, 13.3 million Americans worked in such sales jobs in 2003, selling $25 billion worth of goods. In many cases, like AFLAC, these jobs offer rewards not only for selling the product but for recruiting new people to do so as well. On its dark side, the direct-selling world is filled with costly traps for the unwary—pyramid schemes in which the ultimate product is vague or nonexistent. An outfit called JDO Media, for example, enticed people to make money by enlisting others to sell a sketchily defined "marketing program"—for which privilege each recruit had to put up as much as $3,500.[4]

Even the legitimate firms offer only scant remuneration, with only 8 percent of commission-only salespeople earning more than $50,000 a year and over half earning less than $10,000.[5] Four years ago, an unemployed friend of mine got

3. Peter M. Birkeland, *Franchising Dreams: The Lure of Entrepreneurship in America* (Chicago: University of Chicago Press, 2002), pp. 1–2, 31, 115.
4. Kris Hundely, "Get-Fleeced-Quick," *St. Petersburg Times*, April 12, 2004.
5. Susan B. Garland, "So Glad You Could Come. Can I Sell You Anything?" *New York Times*, December 19, 2004.

drawn into a vitamin-marketing scheme, in which the real rewards, again, came from recruiting others to the sales force. I
went with him to a meeting led by a local doctor, and was impressed by the relative inattention to the vitamins' merits compared to the emphasis on enlisting others to sell them. For his
efforts, my friend lost $400 but gained a vitamin supply that
will hopefully help compensate for his lack of health insurance.

I GET A second "job" offer of the commission-only variety at a
job fair, not long after my success with AFLAC. Mary Kay cosmetics was not one of the companies that attracted me to the
fair,[6] and, when I get there, my impulse is to avoid the Mary
Kay table, which from a distance seems to be loaded with
candy—actually pink cosmetics. But since no potential recruits
are lining up, Linda, the table's minder, is standing in front of
it, and buttonholes me as I loiter in a moment of indecision as
to where to make my next pitch. If I fill out a form, she tells
me, I could win $25 and a free makeover: "Just what you need
when you're looking for a new job!"

She is a large woman in a mauve suit with a white lace top
underneath, mauve eye shadow matching her suit, and a pink
rhinestone pin in the shape of a high heel attached to her
shoulder. Again, I have to wonder why my tasteful silver
brooch was rejected by Prescott, especially if Linda can get
away with this whimsical display. I fill out the form, which
wants only contact information, and reveal that I am looking
for a PR job. "I had a high-up corporate job for thirty-one

6. Internet announcements of job fairs generally offer a list of the "exhibiting"
companies.

years, and one day I realized I was sick of it," she says, her gaze drifting across the room: "The downsizing. Achieving so much and they can never afford a raise. You're up against everyone for promotions. You can't trust anyone. I never got the encouragement from management or the support from other women."

The "support from other women" part holds me rooted in place, trying to imagine this great valentine of a woman in the cutthroat corporate world she's described. Now Linda's problems are solved. "I work only twenty hours a week, and—you know what?—I make as much as I did before." In addition, she works two days a week in a needlepoint shop, "and you know who that is—*women*," in other words, potential Mary Kay customers. "Have you ever used Mary Kay cosmetics?" she asks me.

"No," I admit. "I guess I've been more into L'Oréal."

"That's OK," she says consolingly. "You can say it. You just haven't tried Mary Kay yet."

We set a phone appointment for the following week, and she wishes me "an awesome day." As instructed, I go to the Mary Kay web site and study the wisdom of Mary Kay herself, an elderly woman made up to resemble Dustin Hoffman in *Tootsie.* I learn that high earners can win a pink Cadillac and that the corporate philosophy is "God first, family second, career third." I also talk to Leah Gray, my unemployed acquaintance in Atlanta, because she had put in a stint with Mary Kay.

When you join, there is a miniceremony in a dimly lit room in which the director lights each new consultant's handheld candle and says some encouraging words. I have to admit I thought it was cheesy and overdramatic for my taste. She was saying things like "You've all made the most important life-changing decision: to join Mary Kay." The ironic thing is that I am a very hard sell and fell into this trap.

When we finally connect, Linda is ebullient. "It's a very supportive business. It's awesome. It's hard for me to describe it without sounding like a nutcase."

"What do I need to spend up front?" I ask.

"Just one hundred dollars for the start-up kit, plus thirteen dollars for sales tax and shipping. You can't start any business in this world for just a hundred dollars! Barbara, I am going to get real. I'm sure you've thrown away a hundred dollars for something that's hanging in your closet."

She goes on about how easy it is to learn to do the "skin-care classes" at customers' homes. "I teach you everything and provide you the words to say in the class. They don't care if you read it or memorize it."

It's hard to get a word in edgewise as Linda prattles on, but Leah warned me that she ended up spending over $700 on cosmetics before realizing that this was not for her. So I ask Linda how much I will need to spend on inventory in order to have enough to sell.

"Inventory," she responds meditatively. "I don't usually get that question. Of course, you don't have to buy one ounce. I don't recommend it, though. I suggest eighteen hundred dollars to start. Do you have to? No, but personally this is how I feel. Women don't want to wait for their lipstick and mascara."

So, $1,900 just to get started. "What do you do for health insurance?" I throw in, recklessly.

"You're totally on your own. I have coverage of my own,

which I've had for years. It's a big problem for the country, so it's not just us."

I have gotten the drift now and attempt to cut the call short by claiming an impending appointment. "Look," Linda says in summation, "don't overanalyze this. It's just a fun business and a great opportunity. I can't explain it to you more than that."

SO, AFTER ALMOST seven months of job searching, an image makeover, an expensively refined and later upgraded résumé, and networking in four cities, I have gotten exactly two offers: from AFLAC and Mary Kay. But these are not jobs, not in the way I defined a job when I started this project, in that no salary, benefits, or workplace is provided. Surely there are plenty of actual sales jobs offering a salary and benefits in addition to commissions, but a real job involves some risk taking on the part of the employer, who must make an investment in order to acquire your labor. In real estate, franchising, and commission-only sales, the only risk undertaken is by the job seeker, who has to put out money up front and commit days or weeks to unpaid training. Then she is on her own, ever fearful that the market will soften or that the quasi employer will flood the area with competing sales reps or franchisees.

No one, apparently, is willing to take a risk on me. Is the fear that, if given health insurance for even a month, I will go on an orgy of body scans and elective surgery? The most any corporation seems willing to give me is the right to wear its logo on my chest and go about pushing its products.

I had pictured the corporate world that I seek to enter as a castle on a hill, outside of which the starving vagrants wander, set upon by wolves and barbarian hordes, begging for entry into the safety of the fortified towers. But now I see there is another zone out here: a somewhat settled encampment, where people toil for uncertain rewards at minor tasks invented by the castle dwellers. There is an advantage to occupying this zone: you are free of the rigid conformity required of those who dwell inside; you can actually "Be Your Own Boss!" A few do very well, acquiring pink Cadillacs or fortunes from real estate deals. Many more are ruined or pour themselves into efforts that generate near-poverty-level earnings year after year. There is no safety out here; the wolves keep circling.

eight

Downward Mobility

The fact that I am attending job fairs at all is a measure of my declining expectations. None of my coaches ever recommended job fairs, or even mentioned them, and I got the impression that many are pitched to entry-level workers rather than professionals.[1] On a web site advertising a Los Angeles job fair, I find advice confirming this somewhat downscale orientation:

> Don't forget to wash up before you arrive—you may be nervous, and a little scented soap can mask light perspiration. We recommend avoiding colognes and perfumes, as some people may be allergic. This is probably not the right forum for maximum

1. Outside of college job fairs, organized for graduating seniors, most are organized by companies like JobExpo and advertised on the Internet.

personal expression: try to avoid clothes and jewelry that are gaudy; covering up tattoos is a good idea, as well.

In an environment where people have to be reminded to shower in the morning, I may, with my tan suit and a sufficiently confident manner, just stand out as the dynamic professional I still halfheartedly aspire to become. In fact, there are all kinds of job fairs, some aimed more at entry-level workers, some for professionals, some for both, and some narrowly targeted at a particular industry, like security. And the undeniable advantage of a job fair, compared to an Internet job application, is that you get a moment of face time with someone who is actually employed—a nanosecond chance to make an impression.

I find one promising job fair listed on the web site for the military contractor CACI International, which I was visiting because the alleged involvement of some of CACI's employees in the prisoner abuse at Abu Ghraib seemed to make the company an ideal candidate for my "crisis communications" approach. Its web site urged job applicants to apply in person at the fair in August,* and the web site for the fair itself guaranteed that over 100 other companies would be recruiting there too, some of them, surely, looking for professionals like me.

The fair occurs in Maryland at a cheesy-looking suburban catering joint, where you enter into a two-story-high atrium featuring a giant chandelier, sprays of pink and white fake flowers, and a couple of neoclassical plaster sculptures of partially clad boys holding up light fixtures. Beyond the atrium, there's one of those cavernous spaces cut through with rows of

---

*Most of July was spent on Ehrenreich business.

booths, the kind of scene I associate with the annual book-sellers' convention. There are over 100 booths, from ABC Supply Company to Weichert Realtors, including AFLAC, Home Depot, Men's Wearhouse, as well as government agencies like the Border Patrol, the Air Force Reserve, and the Newport News Police Department. Some of the booths display little souvenirs of their corporations: ballpoint pens, key chains, baggies of golf tees. Many are staffed by people dressed in company logo-ed polo shirts, which suggests they are pretty low-level functionaries, though who knows?

By 10:30 A.M. there must be 500 people crowding the hall, and some booths—the management-consulting firm Booz Allen Hamilton in particular—have attracted long lines. I am, fashion-wise, at the far corporate end of the spectrum, standing out from the many job seekers in casual clothes, even, in some cases, taboo items like tank tops and capris. But class confers no advantage here. The fair, I realize, is the fleshly analog of the Internet job boards, where, instead of sending our résumés to vie for attention, we have come in our actual bodies, to what looks like equally little effect. All "interviews" are conducted standing up; even the people staffing the booths lack chairs—the better to speed up the process. I try to have a copy of my résumé out of my tote bag (I know, it should be a briefcase) and ready to present when I reach the head of the line, along with an eager, but not desperate, smile. Each encounter takes a minute or less, with the conclusion being signaled by a handshake.

For a warm-up I go to the Border Patrol and study the attractive posters showing men on horses. "Will I get to ride a horse?" I ask the uniformed man staffing the booth. He informs me that the maximum age for BP agents is thirty-seven, which I confess to having exceeded some time ago. Then off to Sodexho, a major supplier of campus food services, for a more serious practice run. I shake hands with one of the two men in the booth, then hit him, a little too bluntly, with "You could use some help with PR." The recipient of my handshake looks taken aback, but I forge on: "You're aware of the campus campaign against Sodexho?"[2] Now the other guy raises an eyebrow and admits to having heard of it.

"I could help you with that," I tell them, offering my crisis communications mantra. "You know PR isn't just about lighting fires; it's about putting them out."

I try the same confrontational approach, only a little more smoothly, at CACI. The young woman who is accepting résumés—dressed, I should mention, in a distinctly noncorporate flounced skirt—looks blank at the mention of PR and passes me along to a suited man lurking behind her. The company web site didn't list any PR openings, but that is no barrier to me; the point is to convince them that they need my services whether they realize it or not. I know I have less than sixty seconds to wow this man with my knowledge and skills, so I cut to the chase.

"You might want to rethink your PR approach," I suggest to him as gently as possible, citing CACI's PR director Jody Brown's responses to the allegations of torture in the *New York Times,* which I had studied in advance.

"What did she say?" asks the suit.

"It's a matter of language," I tell him. "She called the alle-

2. Sodexho was first targeted by student activists in the late nineties for its investments in private, profit-making prisons. In 2003, students at a number of colleges relaunched the "Drop Sodexho" campaign in the wake of a bias suit alleging racist management practices.

gations 'irresponsible and malicious.'[3] In other words, she brushed them off. You need gravitas, dealing with these things—like 'We take these charges very seriously and are doing a full investigation, et cetera.' "

He looks actually interested; at least the eye contact lingers, so I rush on. "See, a response like hers can be like pouring gasoline on a fire. One of the functions of skillful PR is to put the fires out."

By now we have gone well past my allotted minute. He takes my résumé and urges me to FedEx, not e-mail, my résumé to Jody Brown.

"Don't tell her what I said, OK?" I ask with a smile as I leave, and when I glance back, he is still following me with his eyes, which should be a good sign but, given the nature of his business, creeps me right out. I hasten toward the coffee table, now thoroughly plundered of refreshments, where, in a rare moment of moral lucidity, I face the fact that my professional flexibility does not extend to defending torture allegations. Jody will be getting no résumé from me.

The CACI interaction, I soon see, was exceptional for its depth and duration. What I am realizing is that most of the company representatives here are not empowered to deal with professionals; they are indeed fishing for frontline, entry-level personnel. At Blackwater, which provides security staff to American companies and civilian personnel in Iraq, two women in Blackwater polo shirts look utterly blank at the term *PR* and quickly resume their trick of chewing gum in unison. At NAID, a provider of "management services in IT,"

3. Kate Zernike, "The Reach of War: Contractors," *New York Times,* June 10, 2004.

I am told that there might be an opening in its Baghdad operation, but that this is not the place to apply for it. I wait in line
after line, leaving résumés at Beta Analytics, Bowhead Support Services, Camber Corporation, Custer Battles ("an international business risk consultancy"), EDO Corporation,
EG&G Technical Services, Independence Air, Inova Health
System, SRA International, Telos Corporation, Unisys, and
Lockheed Martin. Everywhere the response is the same: PR is
a "corporate function" for which I should apply on the company web site.

Most of my attempts to strike up conversations with other
job seekers in line fall flat; we are, after all, competing for the
same limited number of opportunities. In the EDO line,
though, I find myself next to a stoop-shouldered man of about
fifty, whose suit and tie suggest he's a fellow professional. Yes,
he is a manager, a systems manager in fact, and has been searching for four months. "Do you think this is worthwhile?" I ask.

"Well, they just send you to their web site. So I apply on the
web site and call a week later, and they have no idea who I am."

"So there's no point to these job fairs?"

"I go to them anyway." He shrugs. "It makes me feel like
I'm doing something."

THE FAILURE OF the Maryland job fair to net a single positive
response to my follow-up applications at the company web
sites, combined with the perpetual desolation of my in-box,
points to the sorry conclusion that I have been aiming too
high. I blame Kimberly, of course, for encouraging me to imagine myself as a VP of public relations or similarly titled executive. The truth is, I seem to be more like AFLAC material,

which, in terms of real, salaried jobs, would put me somewhere down near the clerical level. So I swallow my executive pride and start thinking of more realistic possibilities. Since I type slowly and lack the software skills now required of secretaries, I apply for a couple of receptionist jobs—again, to no effect. I even pursue a job wanding air travelers with the Transportation Safety Administration, until I note that the penalties for dissimulating to the federal government make that one unworthy of the risk. I resolve to go to another job fair, in a humbler frame of mind, this time—open to anything.

The next job fair, announced on Jobexpo.com, again with no clue as to what sorts of jobs may be offered, turns out to be even more "a complete waste of time," in the words of a young south Indian IT job seeker, than the one in Maryland. Held in the ballroom of a Holiday Inn in Edison, New Jersey, it resembles a high school prom gone horribly wrong: there are only seven companies represented—at tables around the wall rather than booths—and a maximum of thirty job seekers drifting around at any one time. Does the small number of job seekers mean the economy is improving, or does the paucity of potential employers mean that it's worsening? But the configuration of the ballroom, with the employers up against the wall, has a strangely empowering effect on me. They are the wallflowers; I am in the center of the dance floor.

In line with my reduced expectations, I have dropped the difficult "PR" designation and broadened my capabilities to "communications"—or, as I now put it, "anything involving words"—including "speech writing, speech coaching, internal communications, press relations." My first stop is AIL, an insurance company which turns out to be looking for sales reps, and, agreeably enough, the man behind the table invites me to a "group interview" next Wednesday. "10:15 Wen," he writes on a card, proving that this firm could indeed use some help with words or at least abbreviations. At AT&T Wireless, they are also looking for sales reps, though here too a word person might find adequate challenges. The company's blurb in the job fair program reads:

> Are you a Natural? Are you ready to put your skills to work. Like the way you're a quick study. How you're good at finding solutions. And how you're able to relate to people in a professional way.

When I give the AT&T guy my line about how I do "anything with words," he responds, "So you're a people person," and accepts my résumé.

I float from table to table, meeting Mike from Ciber, with whom I chat about crab cakes (he spent his vacation sailing in the Chesapeake Bay), and, once again, some folks from the Border Patrol, who have a lot to say about wines. (Napa gets all the attention, but the Southern California ones are right up there too.) Finally, exhausting my supply of benevolence as well as of tables to approach, I wander into the corridor, where an older African-American woman and light-skinned young man are sitting on one of the backless couches. Neither has bothered with corporate dress; in fact the man daringly sports fringed pants and a rhinestone earring. "Any luck?" I ask them, to rueful looks and exasperated hand waving. "All they want here is salespeople," the guy, who introduces himself as Mark, says. "And I hate sales."

They invite me to sit down between them—"Come on, dear, give those feet a rest"—which is a tight squeeze, bonding me to the older woman at the hip. Mark describes himself as an administrative assistant, but he seems to have done a little of everything: producing promotional videos, fielding complaints from prescription drug users, not to mention PowerPoint and Excel. "I don't want to change the world," he says airily. "Let the CEOs do that. Just give me a job, and I'll get it done." All of his work appears to have come his way via temp agencies. "I guess that's what they want us all to be," I speculate, "temps."

"Right," says the woman, "so they don't have to pay for your insurance."

Mark insists that temping is a good way "to get a foothold" in a company but then contradicts this with a story about how he completed in two months a project that his employer had thought would take six. "They called me in and said 'bye-bye.' I'd worked my way out of the job."

"So maybe you need to slow down a little?" I venture.

"Yeah," adds the woman. "Drag it out a little."

They both break out laughing. I laugh too, and for some reason we can't stop laughing, pressed thigh-to-thigh there on the invisible outer border of corporate America. Even the anxious-looking Asian-American man on the next couch, who has been poring over the list of companies at the fair, joins in with a guilty smile. I am sorry when they have to leave—it emerges that Mark is one of several job seekers on a bus tour of local job fairs provided by the state employment agency, and that his female companion is the bus driver. It occurs to me that in almost a year of searching, this is the first time I have shared a real laugh with a fellow job seeker, and he was far below my imagined "executive" status.

Maybe I should have asked if I could go along with them.

But they mentioned another job fair at the Marriott "right down the street," and I decide to set out for it on foot. The trouble is, there are no sidewalks, this being a kind of diffuse industrial park area, and the slight heels on my shoes keep getting caught in the squishy grass, giving me a tipsy gait. No one walks here except for a few Hispanic men—day laborers, I suppose—and none of them remembers seeing a Marriott around. A light rain develops out of the dirty late-summer sky, speckling my tan suit, and I am about to turn back when a Marriott suddenly emerges on the left. But it's only a Marriott Courtyard, and the front-desk people tell me that any job fair would likely be back at the full-service Marriott in the other direction. So I stumble back past the Holiday Inn to the real Marriott, passing a few more pedestrian representatives of the class that requires muscle instead of résumés. If the corporate world is a fortress, I have been reduced to circling it on foot.

Alas, there is no job fair at the Marriott. Bypassing the front desk and going straight to the ballroom, I find a sign saying "MetLife," a generous buffet lunch spread out in the corridor, and a room full of MetLife functionaries sitting at parallel tables, many still nibbling from their plates. Why not just go in and sit down, as though I am one of them? Take a little rest before staggering back to the Holiday Inn, fantasize that I am employed and valued enough to be sent to an out-of-town meeting? In the French movie *Time Out,* an unemployed white-collar man never reveals his condition to his family. He gets up every morning, pretends to go to work, once even entering a corporate glass tower, where he wanders around with his briefcase, nodding at the busy people he encounters, and relaxing in an armchair in the atrium until he's eventually challenged by a security guard. If you're white and not pushing a shopping cart, you can go almost anywhere.

I fill a plate with a chicken wrap and salads and slide into the seat nearest to the door. The suited woman next to me is too busy multitasking to notice my arrival: watching the Power-Point presentation going on at the front of the room while grinding her jaw and working a hangnail down to a bloody stump. Everyone else seems equally intent on the screen, which reads "Rating and Underwriting Rules and Algorithm, Experience rating spreadsheet, strategies, u/w guidelines." Insofar as I can comprehend the questions and comments, they are discussing how many claims they can reject before they drive the client away. Far more interesting are the toys available on our tables: crayons on mine, crayons plus small containers of Play-Doh at the table in front of us. A man in his fifties has fashioned a kind of pumpkin out of his Play-Doh, with segments in different colors. So this is what it's like on the inside—difficult and scary, yes, but with playful little encouragements to regress.

Then a man comes in the door from the corridor and walks straight up to me. "I'm Mike," he says sotto voce, shaking my hand, "and you are?" When I give him my name, he wants to know where I'm from.

"Communications," I tell him.

"Based where?"

"Uh, Denver."

He gives me a knowing smile and walks off. Why didn't I think to add, after Denver, "We're starting a new project there"? Maybe he thinks I'm a spy from Aetna or Unicare and is about to summon security. I give myself ten more minutes to clean my plate and rest my feet, because the painful truth is: this moment of fantasy employment is as close as I'm ever going to get.

I continue to make applications and follow-up phone calls through September, until I am overwhelmed by a sense of futility. If this were my real life and my actual livelihood were at stake, I would be climbing the walls. But even in my artificial situation as a journalist-slash-job seeker, I cannot help feeling the rejection. All my life, my real life, that is, I've found myself in one strange situation after another, and always managed to succeed or at least survive. Am I not plucky, resourceful, even a wee bit charismatic? The answer, coming in the form of nothing at all—no responses, no nibbles, no interest of any kind— apparently is *not*.

Then, too, I will confess to having looked forward to my climactic and of course entirely voluntary exit from the corporate world. I would work for three or four months, according to the original plan—promoting my company's new libido-enhancing drug or rationalizing the deaths from its painkillers—until I arrived at the *hasta-la-vista* moment when I would suddenly announce to my bewildered employer that I was going on to better things, meaning my actual life. And it *is* better, my freelance freedom, than anything I might find in an office or cubicle—I see that more clearly than ever now. But I can no longer imagine that it is mine entirely by choice. The corporate world has spoken, and it wants nothing to do with me, not even with the smiling, suited, endlessly compliant Alexander version of me.

FOR THOSE WHO can't afford to be fussy about status or pay, there are of course plenty of jobs in America. Hundreds of thousands of immigrants crowd into the country every year to work in lawn maintenance, on construction crews, or as house-cleaners, nannies, and meat packers. Even in the absence of new job creation, high turnover in the low-wage job sector guarantees a steady supply of openings to the swift and the desperate. To white-collar job seekers, these are known as "survival jobs"—something to do while waiting for a "real" job to come along. But this designation may be overly optimistic.

In late September, my job search effectively over, I started trying to track down the job seekers whose cards I had collected for something approaching a serious interview. I told them I was writing an article on white-collar unemployment for a business publication, as a way of earning a little money while I continued my search. (Later, I contacted them again to tell them that the article had grown into a book and would be written under my usual nom de plume, Barbara Ehrenreich.) Eleven people responded; none had found "real" jobs yet; and even those who had been quite guarded in the settings where I originally met them were eager to talk about their strategies, most of which by now included taking survival jobs.

Not every unemployed professional has to contemplate taking a survival job, of course, at least not right away. Many of the people I met during my search had accumulated enough assets in the course of their working life to be able to coast along for a year or more, even while pouring money into coaching and executive-job-search firms. Others used a variety of strategies to stretch out their stay in the middle class. They sent a stay-at-home spouse into the low-wage workforce. They relinquished the perquisites associated with even minor levels of affluence, such as eating out and other entertainments. They sold off cherished possessions at yard sales or auctioned them on eBay; they downsized their living quarters. John Piering, a fifty-two-year-old laid-off IT professional with two small children, described his family's efforts to hang on:

> We limit how often we go out and stopped using the credit cards. Luckily, we have lowish mortgage payments [about $650 a month]. The big problem is utilities. They just go up and up. We cut down on the AC and leave the windows open. We still have cable TV for the kids and high-speed data access for job searching.

Piering's five-year-old had to be taken out of pre-K, which cost $125 a month. He and his wife—who does temp work, "stuffing envelopes"—now divide the child care the same way many working-class couples do: "I do the day shift; she does the night shift."

Unemployment insurance is the first fallback for the laid-off, but it provides only 60 percent of one's former earnings and ends after twenty-six weeks. In 2004, 3.6 million unemployed Americans exhausted their unemployment benefits before finding a job,[4] and when that happens, even the middle-aged often turn to their parents for help. Hillary Meister, a forty-five-year-old with a career in communications, moved back to the town where her parents live when an illness temporarily curtailed her job search. "Without my family," she says, "I'd definitely be on the streets." Steve, the former marketing man who was thinking of learning about wines to qualify for an upscale serving job, is giving up his current $845-a-month apart-

---

4. Leland, "For Unemployed, Wait for New Work Grows Longer."

ment for a room with kitchen privileges: "All I need is a place where I can plug in a computer." Until now, he says, "my family's been helping me out. Otherwise I'd be on the street, literally . . . But they keep saying, 'What's wrong with you? Just take a job, any job.' "

Unfortunately, there is no reliable information on the numbers of former white-collar workers who eventually succumb to this kind of advice. The Bureau of Labor Statistics measures "underemployment" only in terms of one's hours; that is, you are officially underemployed only if you are working part-time and would prefer to work full-time. In March 2004, the unemployment rate was 5.8 percent, while the underemployment rate, measured strictly as involuntary part-time work, was 10 percent. As to the proportion of people employed at low-paying jobs that make no use of their education or established "skill sets," no reliable estimates are available.

I found plenty of people in this situation, though—people who had gone from unemployment to underemployment in the sense of having to work at jobs inappropriate to their skills. Steve, for example, tried Wal-Mart but found that "for a professional, it's tough. They're looking for someone at very little pay, like eight dollars an hour." Now, as mentioned, he's thinking of waiting tables in a fancy restaurant where he might, just possibly, be able to network with his customers. Gary, a former broadcast journalist and PR person, reports that he's now looking for entry-level positions at Best Buy, Circuit City, and Home Depot. Once these men have landed their jobs as waiters or sales "associates," they will no longer be visible, to the federal government, as members of the "unemployed." Case closed, as far as the larger society is concerned—problem solved.

Others of the long-term unemployed sink even lower in status, to the kind of jobs normally undertaken by recent immigrants or the totally uncredentialed. John Piering went from being an IT professional to "working temp—moving furniture, laborer work," whatever he could get. Hillary Meister tried grooming dogs at PetSmart, until her allergies caught up with her. Dean Gottschalk, a forty-one-year-old computer technician, has been driving a limo. Leah Gray, the former marketing executive I met at the Roasted Garlic, has been working at menial jobs since her first layoff in 2001.

> I've done everything from scrub toilets to clean out apartments in this [apartment] complex for eight dollars an hour. I did that for eight months, and the only benefit was that I got twenty pounds lighter from doing it. It gave me a new appreciation for the predominately Hispanic employees who usually do that kind of thing.

Leah's job search has been, at times, dangerously stressful, she wrote me in an e-mail.

> The vast amount of duress has taken a heavy toll on me. I've had a few "first timers." For the first time, I landed in the emergency room and was diagnosed as having a severe panic attack . . . I had to pull over to the side of the road and call 911. My heart started racing, my throat was swelling, my body was numb, my motor skills were so affected that I couldn't keep my hands gripped on the wheel, and I began to shake profusely. It definitely wasn't a pleasant experience. On a second "first timer," I am very embarrassed to admit that I have been getting collection calls for the bills I incurred for treat-

ment which are in the ballpark of $900 . . . My third "first timer" is that I am $73,000 in debt and have $16,000 until my credit cards are maxed out . . . So, I actually joke with people that I wouldn't mind my identity stolen. I wouldn't have to worry about my debt.

When I spoke to Leah in October, she had just started working at a retail chain "standing on [her] feet on concrete all day" for $7.60 an hour and no benefits. She felt she had little choice of jobs this time: "One reason I took [this job] is that I've tried to stay within five miles of where I live because I don't want to waste money on gas."

Wild alternations like these require a degree of flexibility undreamed of by the most creative career coaches. Take the case of Donna Eudovique, an African-American single mother of two, whose eight-year-long search transformed her into a remarkable jack-of-all-trades. When she moved to Georgia in the wake of a divorce, she discovered—as my brother-in-law had in Colorado—that her teaching credentials were useless without an expensive investment in further courses. Since then, she has done just about everything: driven a truck for Georgia Power, sorted mail for UPS, worked in a copy shop, laid tile and hardwood floors. When I talked to her in September, she was doing substitute teaching for $90 a day and, on the days when no subbing job came through, sewing custom-made dresses for sale (no small skill in itself). "When you get to be forty-eight years old," she told me,

you expect to be well-grounded, be able to sit down and know where your money is coming from . . . But I'm just working off my wits . . . I've got children to feed. Yes, I get discouraged, but I'll do whatever I have to to live. I qualified for food stamps, then they stopped. Now I'm trying to get them back.

Health insurance is a long-lost luxury: "I just make sure I stay really healthy"—she laughed—"eat well, take my herbs, and get an annual exam at a clinic where you pay on a sliding scale." When I remarked on her ability to laugh, she said, "It's the least I can do. I don't have any more tears."

The hope, as one sinks into the world of low-paid, menial jobs, is that either the long-awaited e-mail will finally come, offering a more appropriate professional job, or the survival job itself will provide a route to upward mobility. But the survival job may preclude the search for a better job. While I was skeptical about my coaches' insistence that searching is a full-time job in itself, it easily eats hours a day—hours that are no longer available to the survival-job-holder. "It's hard to continue the search with ten- to fourteen-hour work-days," Dean Gottschalk, the tech guy turned limo driver, told me. "I've had to cut back on interviews for now. What I bring in is just a notch above slinging burgers." Steve, who had been about to study wines, has laid-off friends who are working at Home Depot and Lowes, "but they're so tired af-ter lifting all day, they're too tired to do their searching." Leah Gray encountered another problem familiar to the un-employed and underemployed: while she had lost weight do-ing manual labor, the stresses of this last year provoked a thirty-pound gain, and she can't afford to buy a new suit for interviews.

Gary, whose pregnant wife had to give up her job for bed rest shortly after he lost his own job, is optimistic about the possibility of moving up the management ladder within a survival job at one of the big-box stores: "Just getting into the groove again would be good. It could lead to something big. You gotta get a foot in the door. You have to be positive." Similarly, Steve believes that if the job as a server at a fancy restaurant doesn't come through, a barrista job at Starbucks could lead to his becoming a shift supervisor at $10 an hour, although he knows "you have to burn a lot" to achieve that position. What many of the white-collar unemployed don't realize is that their professional expectations and outlook can, perversely, hamper their success in a survival job. John Piering left a job at Radio Shack because he had his own managerial ideas and "didn't like the way they did things." Donna Eudovique was fired from one of her jobs because she refused to abandon her professional image: "The boss came and told me not to dress the way I do—I wear skirts and suits. They told me to wear blue jeans . . . He fires me and tells me it's because of the way I dressed." As Katherine Newman observes in *Falling from Grace*, "Without any guidelines on how to shed the old self, without any instruction or training for the new, the downwardly mobile remain in a social and cultural vacuum."[5] Trained for responsible positions requiring at least a modicum of leadership and innovation, they are unprepared for the sudden loss of status.

And no matter how upbeat they are—no matter how ingenious and flexible—the unemployed and underemployed understand that the clock is always ticking in the background. The longer you are unemployed, the less likely you are to find

5. Newman, *Falling from Grace*, p. 10.

an appropriate job, and entries like "sales associate," "limo driver," or "server" do not make an attractive filling for the growing Gap in one's résumé. At the same time, you are inexorably aging past the peak of occupational attractiveness, which seems to lie somewhere in the midthirties now. Experience is not an advantage; in fact, as Richard Sennett notes of corporate employment, "as a person's experience accumulates, it loses value."[6] So once you fall into the low-wage, survival-job trap, there's a good chance that you will remain there—an unwilling transplant from a more spacious and promising world.

In the midsixties, China's Chairman Mao conducted a vast experiment in sudden downward mobility. As part of his Great Proletarian Cultural Revolution, thousands of managers and professionals—the very people one might have thought would be essential to the nation's economic development— were abruptly sent to the countryside to work alongside the peasants in the fields. The idea, ostensibly, was that the displaced professionals would come to appreciate the backbreaking labor of planting and sowing that their own well-being ultimately depended on, much as Leah Gray came to respect the Hispanic workers whose toil supports the North American economy. But whatever the socially redeeming value of downward mobility, the experience of a "survival job" can be devastating to those who have been groomed to expect far better. Mao's transplants did not become better citizens; in fact many of them were left permanently embittered by their experience. Perhaps even more so, in a society where worth is measured entirely by income and position, downward mobility carries a sense of failure, rejection, and shame.

6. Sennett, *The Corrosion of Character*, p. 94.

I do not follow my fellow job seekers into the world of survival jobs. My great advantage in this project is that I can simply say "game over" and return to my normal work as a writer. My fellow seekers still hang there, suspended above the abyss.

Conclusion

Could I have done better? Looking back on almost a year of job searching, I can find many things to regret. There were weeks when I failed to "update" my résumé on the job boards, that is, to insert some small change, even in the area of punctuation, that would send my résumé back up toward the top of the virtual pile. There were also many instances of incomplete follow-up, where I failed to follow my résumé with a phone call, although this was usually because I could not find the name of an individual to call. It is likely, too, that, encouraged by the ever-positive and proactive Kimberly, I initially aimed too high, defining myself as an "executive" and, in some applications where current salary figures were required, weighing in at an overweening $60,000 to $70,000 a year. And, wisely or not, I failed to utilize services like "résumé blaster" that, for a fee, will send your résumé out to thousands of random companies—to their considerable annoyance, I should think.

With hindsight, I can see the potentially repellent features of my résumé—my upgraded one, that is. In it, I had eliminated the Gap by turning institutions and organizations previously listed as clients of my consultancy into actual employers. Instead of doing event planning on a freelance basis for a major journalism school, for example, I became a visiting professor who taught public relations students, which is actually a little closer to the truth (although I taught essay writing, not PR, and to journalism students). The idea was that I would be far more attractive as a person who had actually held various jobs, rather than one who had merely flitted through on short-term contracts, and, of course, that a teacher should be well qualified to be a practitioner. But my choice of this particular job may have marked my résumé for instant deletion. Only toward the end of my search did I learn, in G. J. Meyer's book *Executive Blues*, of the "academic stench" that can sink a corporate career.[1]

Less mutable qualities, like age, may have worked against me too. My résumé revealed only that I was probably over forty. But even that relatively youthful status could have repulsed many potential employers. Business journalist Jill Andresky Fraser warned me that a forty-plus woman was unlikely to be hired except by someone seeking a "motherly secretary." Katherine Newman, among others, has documented corporate age discrimination, quoting, for example, a Wall Street executive who told her, "Employers think that [if you're over forty] you can't think anymore. Over fifty and [they think] you're

---

1. Meyer tells of a friend whose career at a publishing house hit a dead end, apparently because he had a master's degree in English and had taught for years: "Because of it he never became one of the boys" (p. 169).

burned out."[2] Yet more and more people are working, or seeking work, well into their midfifties and beyond, in part because pensions have become so rare. The Labor Department estimates that workers over fifty-five will make up 19 percent of the workforce in 2012, up from 14 percent in 2002.[3]

Another disadvantage arose from the artificiality of my situation. A normal job seeker of my age would have acquired a Rolodex of contacts to turn to when unemployment hit— people she knew through previous jobs and social contacts in the corporate world. Obviously, I could not turn to friends and ask them to help me go undercover within their firms or to expend their credibility on vouching for me to another firm. Far more than many job seekers, I was on my own and required to carve out new contacts within an alien environment.

But I gave it my best shot. I paid for coaches, I traveled far and wide to networking occasions and executive-job-search training sessions. I underwent a physical makeover and, although perhaps less successfully, attempted to soften my normally blunt persona into something more "likable" and "team player"–like. I spent long days hunched over my computer and working the phone. I read at least a dozen how-to books on networking, interviewing, and self-marketing in general. Yes, I could have given $4,000 to a firm like McCarthy and Company to polish myself even further and introduce me to its networking contacts. But as it was, I spent over $6,000 on my various coaches, trips, training and networking sessions, books, and positions on "elite" or "VIP" job boards. If there were other,

2. Newman, *Falling from Grace*, p. 65.
3. Porter and Walsh, "Retirement Turns into a Rest Stop as Pensions and Benefits Dwindle," *New York Times*, February 9, 2005.

entirely different, tacks to take, none of the job seekers I met seemed to know of them.

It is the existence of so many other luckless job seekers, many of them far more likely to succeed than myself, that makes me believe I probably did not do such a shoddy job of searching after all. Most of the people I met during my search had the advantages of being younger than I am, thoroughly familiar with the corporate world and its expectations, and possessed of relatively Gap-free résumés, at least until their recent bouts of unemployment. They had, in many cases, managed large numbers of people, handled impressive sums of money, nurtured important projects from start to finish—even, in some accounts, won lavish praise before being asked, usually out of the blue, to clean out their desks. Like me, they utilized the job boards, the networking groups, and the executive "transition" sessions. In fact, my guess is that in most cases they were much more disciplined than I was about turning the search into a full-time, home-office-based job. But months later, most of them are no closer to a job than I am.

IN ONE SENSE, though, I was successful. If I did not get through the door, I at least got a taste of white-collar life at its most miserable and precarious. It is not a world I was prepared for, nor, I think, were most of the other job seekers I encountered within it.

Middle-class Americans, like myself and my fellow seekers, have been raised with the old-time Protestant expectation that hard work will be rewarded with material comfort and security. This has never been true of the working class, most of which toils away at wages incommensurate with the effort required. And now, the sociologists agree, it is increasingly untrue of the educated middle class that stocks our corporate bureaucracies. As sociologist Robert Jackall concluded, "Success and failure seem to have little to do with one's accomplishments."[4] Of the unemployed people I met during my search, some were innocent victims of mass purges; others had in fact been ascending in their careers at the time they were ordered to leave. Paul, whom I met at the ExecuNet session, reported being singled out precisely for his high earnings, which reflected prior accomplishments. Leah Gray said she received an adulatory evaluation shortly before being laid off from her last good job. Jeff Clement had been commended for his branch's performance by the COO the very week he was fired.

Capitalism, as Marx observed—with surprising admiration for its dynamism—never promised stability, and it's been a generation since blue-chip companies like IBM offered their white-collar workers a job for life. As the best-seller *Who Moved My Cheese?* advises, dislocated professionals must learn to adapt to new flavors of cheese as the old ones are taken away. But when skilled and experienced people routinely find their skills unwanted and their experience discounted, then something has happened that cuts deep into the very social contract that holds us together.

Bouts of unemployment, if nothing else, provide some time to figure out what it is. People used to working sixty to eighty hours per week, in the office, at home, and while commuting, suddenly find themselves with time on their hands. Time to reflect and ask not only *what would I really like to do?*—the

4. Jackall, *Moral Mazes*, p. 41.

question that the career coaches always urge you to ponder—but, more broadly, *what's wrong with this picture?*

And this effort need not be undertaken alone. People have a natural—I would guess, hardwired—need to reach out to others in similar states of distress. Breast cancer sufferers, gambling addicts, and people squeezed by chronic debt, among others, routinely gather in support groups for comfort and practical tips. And today, perhaps more than at any other time in our history, white-collar victims of corporate instability have opportunities to confront their common problems together. Thanks to the "transition industry," with its many networking events and coaching sessions, the unemployed and the precariously employed can get together on a regular basis, meet, and talk. These events could become settings for a wide-ranging discussion, leading, perhaps, to some kind of action.

But in my experience, no such discussion or action occurs.[5] When the unemployed and anxiously employed reach out for human help and solidarity, the hands that reach back to them all too often clutch and grab. There are the coaches who want $200 an hour for painstakingly prolonged résumé upgrades and pop-psych exhortations. There are the executive-oriented firms that sell office space and contacts doled out one name at a time. And there are, in churches around America, groups that advertise concrete help but have little to offer beyond the consolations of their particular religious sect. In every one of these settings, any potentially subversive conversation about the economy and its corporate governance is suppressed.

---

5. The exception was one meeting of the Washington, D.C., Forty-Plus Club, where pending changes in unemployment insurance were mentioned, though no action was suggested.

I make no claim that this silencing is deliberate. No one has issued an edict warning about the revolutionary threat posed by unemployed and fearful white-collar workers, should they be allowed to discuss their situation freely. But, whatever the motivations of the coaches and organizers of networking sessions, the *effect* of their efforts is to divert people from the hard questions and the kinds of dissent these questions might suggest.

For example, the constant injunction to treat your job search as a job in itself, preferably "supervised" by a friend or a coach, seems designed to forestall seditious musings. Much of the job seeker's "job"—Internet searches and applications—is admitted to be useless, and seems to have no function other than to fill the time that might otherwise be devoted to reflecting on the sources of the problem. Then consider what the coaches advise is a far better use of time than Internet searching: networking. It is networking that creates the possibility of solidarity among the unemployed, the excuse to come together, exchange stories, and perhaps discuss common solutions. But by its very nature networking tends to undercut any incipient solidarity with one's fellow seekers, each of whom is to be regarded at best as a source of contacts or tips, and at worst as a possible competitor.

And even networking was discouraged at many of the events I attended. I was often frustrated to leave a gathering attended by ten to fifty other people knowing hardly anyone's name, occupation, or career trajectory—unless, that is, I managed to snag some fellow participant on the way to the parking lot. Partly this was because most events consisted of such heavy "data dumps"—financial and Internet information, biblical instruction, and so forth—that no time remained for informal socializing. The effect, invariably, was to cut off any serious discussion or exchange of personal experiences. At the networking events and coaching sessions I attended, people often expressed their gratitude to have connected with others in the same boat. "At least now I know I'm not alone" was a common remark. But how little connection was offered!

Finally, consider the constant enjoinder to maintain or develop a "winning attitude." It goes without saying that a smiling, confident person will do better in an interview than a surly one, but the instruction goes beyond self-presentation in particular interactions: you are to actually *feel* "positive" and winnerlike. By the same token, you are to let go of any "negative" thoughts, meaning, among other things, resentments lingering from prior job losses. As one web site I quoted warned, "If you are angry with your former employer, or have a negative attitude, it will show." The prohibition on anger seems unlikely to foster true acceptance or "healing," and it certainly silences any conversation about systemic problems. The aching question— why was I let go when I gave the company so much?—is cut off before it can be asked.

It is not only through the instructions given to job seekers that the transition industry narrows the range of the thinkable and forecloses the possibility of collective action. In books, coaching sessions, and networking events aimed at the white-collar unemployed, the seeker soon encounters ideologies that are explicitly hostile to any larger, social understanding of his or her situation. The most blatant of these, in my experience, was the EST-like, victim-blaming ideology represented by Patrick Knowles and the books he recommended to his boot-camp participants. Recall that at the boot camp, the timid suggestion that there might be an outer world defined by the market or ruled by CEOs was immediately rebuked; there was only us, the job seekers. It was we who had to change. In a milder form, the constant injunction to maintain a winning attitude carries the same message: look inward, not outward; the world is entirely what you will it to be.

On the face of it, the Christian ideology that can be found at so many events run by "career ministries" or eager Christian businessmen is a direct rebuttal of this EST-like philosophy. To Knowles and authors like Mike Hernacki, you alone are responsible for your fate. To the Christians in the job-search business, it is God who takes sole responsibility. Hernacki recognizes the conflict: "In the past, when I've expressed this message, some people have reacted angrily and said that this somehow denies the existence of God as the Source." But he nimbly resolves it by observing, "If you believe God is the Source, and the Source is on your side, working through you, you don't have an excuse to plead helplessness again."[6] In other words, prayer gives the believer access to the same kind of infinite power Hernacki exercises through his thoughts. Different as they seem on the surface, the atheistic philosophy of individual will and the distorted Christianity I encountered both offer the fantasy of omnipotence. And if you can achieve anything through your own mental efforts—just by praying or concentrating hard enough—there is no need to confront the social and economic forces shaping your life.

SUPPOSE THAT THE transition zone encouraged free-ranging discussion. What might the topics of conversation be? For a

---

6. Hernacki, *The Ultimate Secret to Getting Absolutely Everything You Want,* pp. 55–56.

start, people might want to address the question of what is happening in the corporate world today; in particular, why does experience seem to be so little valued and accomplishment so unreliably rewarded? Some may object that *the corporate world* is a vague abstraction, concealing a rich diversity of environments, but it was in common use among my fellow job seekers, who often expressed hopes of escaping from it—into a small business, for example, or what they saw as a more meaningful form of work. In saying that I was searching for a corporate position, I seemed to be moving in the opposite direction from many of my fellow seekers, who often expressed a strong desire to get out.

"Companies are colder these days" is how Hillary Meister put it. "There's no sense of stability anymore. A lot has to do with greed." Donna Eudovique echoed her: "It's so cold-blooded now. There's no warning, no thanks, just 'take your stuff and don't come back tomorrow.'" For all that they missed their salary and benefits, no job seeker I met ever expressed nostalgia for the camaraderie of the workplace, perhaps because they had experienced so little of it. In her most recent job, one of my informants felt she had been marked for firing almost from day one, when she unwillingly confessed to having been treated for cancer. During the interviews, everyone had been friendly, but after learning of her illness, they started making her life "a living hell":

> It was weird. They were like avoiding me. I think they were looking for every tiny mistake . . . They didn't have an orientation. They didn't want me asking for feedback.

Jeff Clement, who had worked in IT staffing and sales, told me:

I'm bitter and cynical about corporate America because I've seen far too many decisions just based on the bottom line. It's not just Enron and WorldCom. I honestly think I lost my last job over ethics. I had someone actually ask me: "Are your values worth more than your paycheck?" They think you can be evil all day and then go home and live the American dream.

Corporations cannot of course offer a completely stable and nurturing environment for their employees: businesses fail; consumer tastes change; technology marches along. The cheese, in other words, is always moving. But we do expect corporations to provide jobs; at least that is the rationale given for every corporate tax cut, public subsidy, or loosening of regulations. The most recent corporate tax break, for example, is provided by the appealingly titled American Jobs Creation Act, although it does nothing at all to encourage job creation. Elected officials coddle the corporations for *our* sake, we are always told; there is no other way to generate jobs.

Once, not so many decades ago, the job-generating function ranked higher among corporate imperatives. CEOs were more likely to stand up to the board of directors and insist on retaining employees rather than boosting dividends in the short-term by laying people off. Appalled by the mass layoffs in her family's firm, Claire Giannini, daughter of the founder of the Bank of America, recalled the days when "executives took a pay cut so that the lower ranks could keep their jobs."[7] A corporation may be a "person" under the law, but we

7. Quoted in Alan Downs, *Corporate Executions: The Ugly Truth About Layoffs—How Corporate Greed Is Shattering Lives, Companies, and Communities* (New York: AHACOM, 1995), p. 31.

understand it to be composed of many hundreds or thousands of actual people—which is what makes it *corporate* in the original sense of the word.

It is the corporate, or collective, aspect of corporations that has fallen into disrepair. There are two legal ways to make money: by increasing sales or by cutting costs. In most cases, a corporation's highest operating expense is its payroll, making it a tempting target for cuts. In addition, the mergers and acquisitions that so appeal to CEO egos inevitably result in layoffs, as the economies of scale are realized. Or downsizing may be undertaken as a more or less routine way of pleasing the shareholders, who, thanks to stock options, now include the top-level managers.

So, by eliminating other people's jobs, top management can raise its own income. The trend was clear in the midnineties: CEOs who laid off large numbers of employees were paid better than those who didn't.[8] In the last few years, outsourcing has reaped the greatest rewards for CEOs: compared to other firms, compensation has increased five times faster at the fifty U.S. firms that do the most outsourcing of service jobs.[9]

Put in blunt biological terms, the corporation has become a site for internal predation, where one person can advance by eliminating another one's job. In his business advice book *QBQ!* (which stands, mysteriously, for "the question behind the question"), John G. Miller quotes "a senior leader of a financial institution":

8. Downs, *Corporate Executions,* p. 28.
9. John Cavanagh, Sarah Anderson, Chris Hartman, Scott Klinger, and Stacy Chan, *Executive Excess 2004: Campaign Contributions, Outsourcing, Unexpensed Stock Options, and Rising CEO Pay,* available at www.faireconomy.org.

Sometimes people say to me, "I don't want to take risks." I tell them, "You and I had better take risks, because there are about a dozen people at their computers right now in this building trying to eliminate our jobs!"[10]

And the management consultant David Noer observes:

Organizations that used to see people as long-term assets to be nurtured and developed now see people as short-term costs to be reduced . . . [T]hey view people as "things" that are but one variable in the production equation, "things" that can be discarded when the profit and loss numbers do not come out as desired.[11]

There are limits of course to this kind of Darwinian struggle. At some point the survivors will no longer be able to absorb the work of those who have been eliminated, no matter how hard they try.

So another question that the unemployed and the precariously employed might want to take up is: Is this any way to do business? Some management consultants, while urging acceptance of the seemingly inevitable demise of the "old paradigm" based on mutual loyalty between the company and its employees, nevertheless argue that the "lean and mean" trend ultimately undermines the business, as more and more work is left to the exhausted, insecure survivors.

10. John G. Miller, *QBQ! The Question Behind the Question: What to Really Ask Yourself to Eliminate Blame, Complaining, and Procrastination* (New York: G. P. Putnam's Sons, 2004).
11. David Noer, *Healing the Wounds: Overcoming the Trauma of Layoffs and Revitalizing Downsized Organizations* (San Francisco: Jossey-Bass, 1993), p. 17.

• • •

WHEN THEY REACH out for help, the unemployed enter an insidiously manipulative culture—one that was utterly foreign to me. I have some acquaintance with another kind of institutional culture—that of the university—and had expected the corporate culture to be very different, with far less wasted effort, for example, in the form of tradition or self-indulgent personality conflicts. I expected, as I approached the corporate world, to enter a brisk, logical, nonsense-free zone, almost like the military—or a disciplined, up-to-date military anyway—in its focus on concrete results. How else would companies survive fierce competition? But what I encountered was a culture riven with assumptions unrelated to those that underlie the fact- and logic-based worlds of, say, science and journalism—a culture addicted to untested habits, paralyzed by conformity, and shot through with magical thinking.

Of course, I was never officially accepted into the corporate world as a regular employee, but I have every reason to believe that the transition zone occupied by the unemployed offers a fairly accurate glimpse into its culture. For one thing, the individuals who provide coaching, who lead group sessions and facilitate networking events, are for the most part themselves veterans of the corporate world. In addition, many transition enterprises serve not only the unemployed, but corporate clients as well, providing counseling and pep sessions for current executives and other professionals. Hence the ideology and expectations of the transition industry cannot be too far out of line from those of the corporate culture at large—and much of what I found there was disturbingly loony.

The reliance on empirically baseless personality tests, for example, and the deeper assumption that humans can be sorted into nine or so distinct "personality types," echo the medieval notion of "humors"—"choleric," "bilious," et cetera—determining mood and health. Then there's the almost numerological faith that things have been clarified once they have been organized into categories and counted, as in the "seven habits," the "four competencies," "the sixty-four principles of success." Lists may be useful as a mnemonic device, but they are not an analytic tool and, whether the subject is chemistry or marketing, do little to illuminate the world.

Perhaps the strangest aspect of the corporate world as I encountered it was the constant emphasis on "personality" and "attitude." In the world of journalism, as in the academy, quirky, even difficult, people are commonplace, and no one complains as long as the copy gets in on time or the students master the subject matter. But the path to the corporate world is lined with admonitions to upgrade or improve one's personality. Coaches administered personality tests and talked about the importance of being upbeat and likable; Internet and book-based advice urged a thorough retuning of one's attitude; networking events emphasized the necessity of staying "up." Other job searchers agreed that success depends on one's ability to conform to the immediate microculture. As Hillary Meister put it: "If they find someone who gets along with them and who has the right personality, they'll like them. In an interview today, chemistry matters more than skills." Jeff Clement attributed success to

> personality, who you knew. If the boss was into golf, we were all supposed to be into golf. If he smoked cigars, we all

smoked cigars. If he drank brandy, we all had to drink brandy. Eventually you saw some serious vices and then you had something on him. Then, if you have the dirt on them, they'll keep you on. To survive, you need to know where the bodies are buried.

What does personality have to do with getting the job done? I am still confident that I could have been, as Kimberly put it, a "crackerjack PR person," at least as far as job performance goes. But could I have played the requisite role, as prescribed by the coaches and gurus? The rationale commonly given for the emphasis on personality is that today's corporate functionaries are likely to work in "teams," within which one's comportment and demeanor are at least as important as one's knowledge and experience. Yet despite the personality tests, which rest on the assumption that personalities vary from person to person, only one kind of personality seems to be in demand, one that is relentlessly cheerful, enthusiastic, and obedient—the very qualities fostered by the transition industry. Even at the higher levels of management, where you might think there would be room for the occasional disagreeable person—as Enron's Jeffrey Skilling or AOL's Robert Pittman appear to have been—niceness is supposed to prevail. A recent article in the *Financial Times* points out that the requisite personality traits even trump intelligence, and do so at all levels of the corporation.

> Think what characterises the really intelligent person. They can think for themselves. They love abstract ideas. They can look dispassionately at the facts. Humbug is their enemy. Dissent comes easily to them, as does complexity. These are traits that are not only unnecessary for most business jobs, they are

actually a handicap when it comes to rising through the ranks of large companies.[12]

Worse, from my perspective, the same article tells of a woman in a senior position who was upbraided for revealing, in a personality test: "Irony is one of my favourite forms of humour." "She is not going to be fired," the article reports, "but it has been made clear to her that unless she seriously rethinks her sense of humour she might fit better somewhere else."

It is a strange team in which everyone is equally good-natured, agreeable, and not too threateningly bright. In my own experience of group projects there is always at least one, and possibly more, irascible or cynical team member. In fact, it is his or her presence that requires the others to possess the "people skills" that are so valued in the corporate world. Besides, at a time when corporations are supposedly striving for "diversity"—forming "diversity committees" and hiring "diversity specialists"—it seems counterproductive to bar diversity in personality. It can only hinder the achievement of more familiar forms of diversity along the lines of race, gender, and ethnicity. The African-American who is deemed overly sensitive to racial slights, or the woman who speaks out against sexist practices, may be just what the company needs if it is ever to achieve true demographic diversity. But he or she risks being dismissed for failing to be a sufficiently compliant "team player."

Despite all my putative personality defects—sarcasm, impatience, and possibly also intelligence—I did take the rhetoric of "team work" very seriously. The cover letters that accom-

12. Lucy Kellaway, "Companies Don't Need Brainy People," *Financial Times*, November 22, 2004.

panied my job applications always emphasized my desire to work collaboratively, in a "dynamic team," and to enjoy the camaraderie of working with others in a long-term effort "to advance the company brand and image." I had been "consulting" as an individual, and now I was eager to come in from the cold. What I was failing to notice was that my fellow job seekers had been "team members" once themselves, meaning that these must be very fragile "teams" indeed.

For all the talk about the need to be a likable "team player," many people work in a fairly cutthroat environment that would seem to be especially challenging to those who possess the recommended traits. Cheerfulness, upbeatness, and compliance: these are the qualities of subordinates—of servants rather than masters, women (traditionally, anyway) rather than men. After advising his readers to overcome the bitterness and negativity engendered by frequent job loss and to achieve a perpetually sunny outlook, management guru Harvey Mackay notes cryptically that "the nicest, most loyal, and most submissive employees are often the easiest people to fire."[13] Given the turmoil in the corporate world, the prescriptions of niceness ring of lambs-to-the-slaughter.

And even as I write, the bar is being raised. Likability and enthusiasm are no longer enough to make one's personality attractive; just in the past few months, I've noticed more and more demands for *passion*. The advice-meister Stephen Covey, who wrote the 1979 best-seller *The 7 Habits of Highly Effective People,* has come out with an "eighth habit," explaining that

> being *effective* . . . is no longer optional in today's world—it's the price of entry to the playing field. But surviving, thriving, in-

13. Mackay, *We Got Fired!* p. 105.

novating, excelling and leading in this new reality will require us to build on and reach beyond effectiveness. The call and need of a new era is for *greatness*. It's for *fulfillment, passionate execution,* and *significant contribution.*[14] [Covey's italics.]

Increasingly, company web sites offer breathless claims of "passion" as one of their corporate attributes and requirements for employment, as in, "If you are an enthusiastic, creative, passionate person looking for a place where your ideas will be valued, look no further than Delphi." Kevin Craine's online business commentary, "Weekly Insight," advises businesspeople to acquire ". . . passion. You must believe in your strategy and feel passionate about it." *USA Today* observes that:

. . . it's widely accepted that the winning companies during the next generation will be those that have employees come to work and bring with them their hearts, minds, creativity and passion.[15]

Energy and commitment are so 1995; in the twenty-first century one is required to feel, or at least evince, an emotional drive as consuming as romantic love. Before we swoon at the possibilities, though, Covey reminds us that the appropriate level of passion sometimes needs to be whipped up by force. How do you achieve "a united, cohesive culture" in your corporation? "Induce pain," he answers: "As long as people are

14. Stephen R. Covey, *The Eighth Habit: From Effectiveness to Greatness* (New York: Free Press, 2004), p. 4.
15. Del Jones, "Best Friends Good for Business," *USA Today,* December 1, 2004.

contented and happy, they're not going to do much. You don't want to wait until the market induces pain, so you have to induce it in other ways."[16]

The new insistence on "passion" marks a further expansion of the corporate empire into the time and the spirit of its minions. Once, white-collar people were expected to have hobbies; in fact it would have been odd not to cite one in an interview, even if it were only reading or bridge. Today's "passionate" employees, however, are not expected to have the time or the energy for such extraneous pursuits; they are available at all hours; they forgo vacations; they pull all-nighters; they stretch to the limits of their physical and mental endurance. Scientists, writers, and political campaign operatives sometimes do the same, but not for years on end, and not for ever-changing goals.

It is the insecurity of white-collar employment that makes the demand for passion so cruel and perverse. You may be able to simulate passion, or even feel it, for one job, but what about the next job, and the next? Not even prostitutes are expected to perform "passionately" time after time, and of course their encounters seldom end in rejection. Picking up after a firing and regrouping in a mode of passionate engagement, and doing so time after time—this is a job for a professional actor or for a person who has lost the capacity for spontaneous feeling.

OTHER WHITE-COLLAR occupational groups—doctors, lawyers, teachers, and college professors—have done better at carving

16. Covey, *The Eighth Habit*, p. 4.

out some autonomy and security for themselves. Their principal strategy, undertaken in the early twentieth century, was
professionalization: the erection of steep barriers to the occupation, backed up by the force of law and the power of professional organizations like the AMA.[17] No one can practice
medicine, for example, without a thorough education and a li-
cense, nor can a physician—or a professor, for that matter—be
fired without cause. To the strategy of professionalization,
some occupations added the further protection afforded by
unions: teachers, college professors, journalists—even some
physicians—have banded together, much like steelworkers or
miners, to defend themselves against arbitrary and autocratic
employers.

The "business professions," on the other hand, are so called
mainly as a matter of courtesy. Management, for example,
made a relatively late entry into the college curriculum; and
even today, although the MBA has been the fastest-growing
graduate degree for the past two decades, it is by no means a
requirement for a management job.[18] A current TV commercial even mocks MBAs as snotty young know-it-alls who are
helpless in the face of a copying machine. Among the business
"professions," only accounting has the traditional hallmarks of
a profession: legally enforced educational requirements, li-
censing, and a recognized body of knowledge. In the case of
management, human relations, marketing, and PR, anyone

---

17. Professionalization was not entirely a progressive development. As I ar-
gued in *Fear of Falling: The Inner Life of the Middle Class* (New York: Pan-
theon, 1989), the educational requirements for entry into medicine, the "model
profession," were created in no small part to exclude women, minorities, and
people from the lower classes.
18. Rakesh Khurana, Nitin Nohria, and Daniel Penrice, "Is Business Management a Profession?" SearchCIO.com, February 22, 2005.

with a college degree—myself, for example—can present themselves as a potential practitioner. And with this openness comes a huge vulnerability for the veterans in the field: there is no transparent way to judge their performance, and no protection from capricious firings.

But there is something even more central than job security that white-collar corporate workers lack—and that is dignity. A physician sells his or her skills and labor; so, in fact, does the blue- or pink-collar worker. Both the warehouse worker unloading trucks and the engineer designing a bridge can reasonably expect their jobs to involve a straightforward exchange of labor for wages. As the young temp worker I met at the New Jersey job fair put it, "Just give me a job, and I'll get it done." Not so for the white-collar corporate employee, who must sell—not just his skill and hard work—but *himself*. He may wear a "power suit" and look down on the army of more menial workers below him, but he—or she—faces far more intrusive psychological demands than a laborer or clerk would likely countenance. His is a world of intrigue and ill-defined expectations, of manipulation and mind games, where self-presentation—as in "personality" and "attitude"—regularly outweighs performance.

The failure of white-collar corporate workers to band together and defend their jobs and their professional autonomy is usually attributed to their individualism—or to an unwarranted faith in the meritocratic claims of our culture. But physicians, journalists, and even many blue-collar workers are no less likely to be individualistic believers in meritocracy. What sets the white-collar corporate workers apart and leaves them so vulnerable is the requirement that they identify, absolutely and unreservedly, with their employers. While the physician or scientist identifies with his or her profession, rather than with the hospital or laboratory that currently employs them, the white-collar functionary is expected to express total fealty to the current occupants of the "C-suites." As my "crisis management" instructor, Jim Lukaszewski, made clear: the CEO may be a fool; the company's behavior may be borderline criminal—and still you are required to serve unstintingly and without the slightest question. Unfortunately, as the large numbers of laid-off white-collar workers show, this loyalty is not reliably reciprocated.

SO THE UNEMPLOYED continue to drift through their shadowy world of Internet job searches, lonely networking events, and costly coaching sessions. The tragedy is that they could be doing so much more. They could, most obviously, be lobbying for concrete improvements in the lives of the unemployed and anxiously employed. Topping the list would have to be an expansion of current unemployment benefits to a level more like that in the northern European countries, which offer a variety of benefits extending potentially for years. The entire debate about outsourcing, for example, would take a dramatically different and perhaps less nativist tone if American workers had an adequate safety net to fall back on. As it is, the IT person who is required to train her Indian replacement—a not uncommon indignity—might as well be digging her own grave.

Almost as urgent is the need for a system of universal health insurance that is not tied in any way to your job. When people were likely to have three or four jobs in a lifetime, it might have made more sense to leave health insurance to the employers. But as the number of jobs per lifetime rises into the double digits, employer-provided insurance leads to long periods without coverage—with the chance, especially among the middle-aged, that a "prior condition" could come along and disqualify you from further individual coverage, or even from a job. Furthermore, the cost of health insurance has become a major disincentive to job creation; companies would rather outsource or hire benefit-less "contract workers" than take on the burden of providing insurance for new hires. There are eight million unemployed people, of all occupational levels, in America; imagine the effect they might have if they launched a concerted campaign for publicly sponsored universal health insurance.

If an expansion of benefits seems unlikely or even utopian in the current political climate, there is still the immediate challenge of self-defense. On many fronts, the American middle class is under attack as never before. For example, the 2005 federal bankruptcy bill, which eliminates the possibility of a fresh start for debt-ridden individuals, will condemn more and more of the unemployed and underemployed to a life of debt peonage. Meanwhile, escalating college costs threaten to bar their own children from white-collar careers. And as company pensions disappear, the president is campaigning vigorously to eviscerate Social Security. No group is better situated, or perhaps better motivated, to lead the defense of the middle class than the unemployed—assuming they could recognize their common interests and begin to act as a political force.

They have the time, for one thing—not endless hours, since job searching does require some sustained effort, but far more than their counterparts in the workplace, many of whom put in sixty or more hours a week. They also have, in many cases, skills unavailable to the blue-collar unemployed: administrative and computer-related experience, as well, presumably, as the ability to work out a plan or strategy and implement it. And, as living representatives of middle-class decline, they surely have the motivation. If anyone can testify credibly to the disappearance of the American dream, it is the white-collar unemployed—the people who "played by the rules," "did everything right," and still ended up in ruin.

Yes, it will take a change in attitude, a psychological transformation, to make the leap from solitary desperation to collective action. But this is not the kind of transformation the career coaches envision. What the unemployed and anxiously employed need is not "likability" but the real ability to reach out to others and enlist them in a common project, ideally including very different others, like the chronically stressed lower-level workers. What they need, too, is not a "winning attitude" but a deeper and more ancient quality, one that I never once heard mentioned in my search, and that is courage: the courage to come together and work for change, even in the face of overwhelming odds.

acknowledgments

I thank Diane Alexander, Leah Gray, and Kelley Walker for their invaluable research assistance. Diane Alexander, Shakoor Aljuwani, Rosa Brooks, Ben Ehrenreich, and Frances Fox Piven read early drafts and offered extremely useful comments. Jared Bernstein, Heather Boushey, Corinne Coen, John Ehrenreich, Doug Henwood, Ken Hudson, Robert Jackall, and Jerry M. Newman answered assorted questions along the way. Arlie Hochschild and Kris Dahl, who is my agent, took time for long conversations on issues raised by my research. And I'm grateful to the team at Metropolitan Books, including John Sterling for his careful reading, Riva Hocherman for her excellent suggestions, and especially my brilliant editor, Sara Bershtel.

about the author

BARBARA EHRENREICH is the author of thirteen books, including the *New York Times* bestsellers *Nickel and Dimed* and *The Worst Years of Our Lives*, as well as *Blood Rites* and *Fear of Falling*, which was nominated for a National Book Critics Circle Award. A frequent contributor to *Harper's Magazine* and a columnist for *The Progressive*, she has been a columnist at the *New York Times* and *Time*.